Loved

A Play

Olwen Wymark

Samuel French – London
New York – Sydney – Toronto – Hollywood

© 1980 BY OLWEN WYMARK

This play is fully protected under the Copyright Laws of the British Commonwealth of Nations, the United States of America and all countries of the Berne and Universal Copyright Conventions.

All rights, including Stage, Motion Picture, Radio, Television, Public Reading, and Translation into Foreign Languages, are strictly reserved.

No part of this publication may lawfully be transmitted, stored in a retrieval system, or reproduced in any form or by any means, electronic, mechanical, photocopying, manuscript, typescript, recording, or otherwise, without the prior permission of the copyright owners.

Rights of Performance by Amateurs are controlled by SAMUEL FRENCH LTD, 26 SOUTHAMPTON STREET, LONDON WC2E 7JE, and they, or their authorized agents, issue licences to amateurs on payment of a fee. **It is an infringement of the Copyright to give any performance or public reading of the play before the fee has been paid and the licence issued.**

Licences are issued subject to the understanding that it shall be made clear in all advertising matter that the audience will witness an amateur performance; that the names of the authors of the plays shall be included on all announcements and on all programmes; and that the integrity of the author's work will be preserved.

The Royalty Fee indicated below is subject to contract and subject to variation at the sole discretion of Samuel French Ltd.

Basic fee for each and every
    performance by amateurs   Code L
    in the British Isles

In Theatres or Halls seating Six Hundred or more the fee will be subject to negotiation.

In Territories Overseas the fee quoted above may not apply. A fee will be quoted on application to our local authorized agent, or if there is no such agent, on application to Samuel French Ltd, London.

The Professional Rights in this play are controlled by HARVEY UNNA & STEPHEN DURBRIDGE LTD., 14 Beaumont Mews, Marylebone High Street, London W1N 4HE.

The publication of this play does not imply that it is necessarily available for performance by amateurs or professionals, either in the British Isles or Overseas. Amateurs and professionals considering a production are strongly advised in their own interests to apply to the appropriate agents for consent before starting rehearsals or booking a theatre or hall.

ISBN 0 573 11247 9

LOVED

First produced at The Bush Theatre, London, by The Wakefield Tricycle Company, October 26th, 1978, with the following cast of characters:

Amy	Priscilla Morgan
Lawrence	Philip Lowrie
Cissy	Jill Dixon
Arthur	Sean Scanlon
Gabriel	Michael Johnson
Zoe	Veronica Quilligan

Directed by Ken Chubb

First produced in the U.S.A. at Syracuse Stage Theatre, Syracuse, New York, April 20th, 1979, with the following cast of characters:

Amy	Dina Merrill
Lawrence	Richard Abernethy
Cissy	Le Clanché du Rand
Arthur	Jeffrey Ware
Gabriel	Tom Keena
Zoe	Nancy Mette

Directed by Arthur Storch

Time—the present
Place: London

Various settings to represent:
A rather elegant living-room
A garden
Arthur's room

Please note our NEW ADDRESS:

Samuel French Ltd
52 Fitzroy Street London W1P 6JR
Tel: 01 - 387 9373

AUTHOR'S NOTE

The play was originally written for open staging in a very small acting area. The subsequent production in the U.S.A. was presented on a large proscenium stage where it was possible to eliminate the device of Amy and Arthur carrying furniture off and on. The other staging devices, however, were retained as integral to the play. Arthur and Zoe are intended to be real people although they also perform the functions of instigators and, as it were, "guardians". They both speak cockney (not broad) and Arthur should be dressed in unspecific working man's clothes, e.g. faded tan trousers and a worn short raincoat or working jacket.

ACT I

A rather elegant living-room

Amy, resembling an old woman tramp with wild, grey hair, is dressed in a woollen hat; a bulky, ragged, army coat; dirty sneakers, and wears steel-rimmed glasses. She is carrying a dirty, bulging, plastic bag and a stick. As she roams around the room with an exaggerated limp she mutters to herself, touching things with her stick

Amy Oh yes! Oh yes! Bastards! You listen to me. (*She picks up a little vase with a rose in it*) Filth! (*She puts it down in disgust*) Think you're so clever, don't you? You think I don't know, eh? Think I don't know! (*She goes and sits hunched up in a chair*) Just be careful, that's all. Be careful. I can see you. Oh yes.

The telephone rings

(*She starts violently*) What's that what's that what's that? (*She moans and rocks herself in the chair*) Leave me alone. Leave me alone. (*She pushes herself out of the chair and limps over to the telephone. Making a sort of growling noise, she raises her stick threateningly as if she means to smash the telephone, then she drops the stick and picks up the receiver; in a pleasant, cultivated voice*) Oh-one-three-eight.... Yes it is.... Yes, sorry, I was in the bath actually.... No, no, no, not at all.... No, he's not here.... I've no idea I'm afraid.... A message? Of course.... Yes, I've got a pencil. (*Without writing anything*) Yes, yes, I've written that down.

Lawrence (*off*) Amy? Amy!

Amy Yes, I'll tell him the moment I see him.... Yes, yes, I've put down urgent. Good-bye. (*She replaces the receiver*)

She takes a step or two in the direction of Lawrence's voice then changes her mind and scuttles out

Lawrence comes in

Lawrence Was that the 'phone? (*Looking round*) Oh. (*He stands indecisively*) I suppose I could... (*He goes towards the door where Amy went out*) Amy? Are you up there? (*After a pause*) No. Or perhaps yes, of course. Impossible to say. (*Disconsolately*) Oh God. (*After a pause*) I don't know. (*With irritation*) How should I know. (*He sits; depressed*)

Cissy comes on wearing an apron

Cissy (*murmuring to herself*) Hello, Amy, you're back. How lovely.

Hooray. (*Seeing Lawrence*) Oh. Lawrence. I didn't ... I thought you were in the study. I had the feeling I could hear the radio.
Lawrence (*smiling*) I was. In the study. Listening to the radio.
Cissy Oh, well then I . . . Yes.
Lawrence I was listening to the Wednesday Afternoon Play.
Cissy (*with exaggerated interest*) Were you really? Was it good?
Lawrence (*smiling*) I have no idea.
Cissy Ah. Yes. Well. They do wash over one, don't they?

Lawrence remains silent

I find that. (*After a pause she continues brightly*) Well! (*After a pause*) Actually I only came up to . . . (*She stops*)
Lawrence Yes?
Cissie (*hurriedly*) Oh nothing really. No reason at all. Just . . . popped up, you know.
Lawrence Yes.
Cissy I've . . . er . . . made a sort of casserole. Well, when I say sort of . . . (*She presses on*) I got it out of a book called "High Adventure in the Kitchen". (*Doubtfully*) I'm sure it'll be all right. I did think . . . pineapple? Well, with kidneys it did seem a bit . . . (*Quickly with desperation*) Is she back?
Lawrence Who, Amy? I don't really know. She may be. (*Smiling and nodding*) She may easily be.
Cissy Yes, of course. You're right. (*Nervously hearty*) And if she isn't yet she will be soon. Well, I'd better go and look at my casserole. (*She starts out and then stops*) I hope he's not a vegetarian. Though there are baby carrots. And the pineapple, of course. (*Imploringly*) Lawrence, couldn't we telephone him and tell him not to come?
Lawrence (*smiling*) We can't do that, Cissy. We haven't got his 'phone number . . .
Cissy We could try Directory Enquiries.
Lawrence (*smiling*) . . . Or his last name.
Cissy (*sagging*) Yes. (*Resolutely cheerful once more*) Well, he may not come. He didn't come the last time she asked him, after all. So he may not.
Lawrence (*smiling*) Absolutely.

Cissy smiles back at him and starts towards the door again. Lawrence closes his eyes and leans back in the chair

Cissy (*turning back*) There is one thing, Lawrence . . .
Lawrence (*without opening his eyes*) Could it wait do you think, Cissy? I'm rather busy.
Cissy Oh sorry. Of course. Yes. (*She starts out again and then stops*) It's only that when she asked me to come and live here and do the cooking . . . Amy knows I can't cook!
Lawrence Nonsense, Cissy. You mustn't underestimate yourself.
Cissy (*going over to Lawrence*) I don't underestimate myself, Lawrence,

Act I

I assure you. Please don't feel that you'd hurt my feelings by being truthful.
Lawrence But Cissy, I . . .
Cissy No, no. My *amour propre* doesn't come into play *vis-à-vis* the cooking. It's difficult for me to know sometimes when it does . . . Come into play. However, hand on heart, Lawrence (*Putting her hand on her heart*) the truth would not injure me. I can't cook. I never have been able to and I never will be, I'm afraid. I think it's something missing from my nature.
Lawrence Now, Cissy, you . . .
Cissy Naturally I feel regret, even shame because of the expense. (*With some passion*) Lawrence, I've been here a month now. How many nights have there been when one of us has not had to go out and fetch food from the take-away?
Lawrence Several, surely. We . . .
Cissy Only the nights when we've had cold meat and salad which no-one could honestly call cooking. Even then, the time I took a chance on hardboiling some eggs the yolks came out blue. Lawrence, I know she's my own sister and I wouldn't dream of saying anything against her but where does she go? What does she do? What are we to think?

Amy comes on wearing a flowered dress

Hello, Amy, you're back. How lovely. Hooray.
Amy Hello, Cissy. Hello, Lawrence, you look tired.
Lawrence (*springing up*) No, no. No, no, no.
Amy Oh good.

The three stand smiling at each other. Amy is genuinely cordial, Lawrence and Cissy are slightly rigid

Cissy What a pretty dress. Is it new?
Amy Yes. It's a little too long, I think.
Cissy (*intently*) Yes. Yes, perhaps you're right.
Amy What do you think, Lawrence?
Lawrence Well . . . (*He stands back and looks at her*) Yes. A shade too long. Yes.

They all smile at each other as before

Amy What are we having for supper, Cissy?
Cissy Kidneys. And baby carrots.
Amy Delicious.
Cissy And pineapple. And there are raisins. And there's cream in it. The seasoning is called turmeric. I had to go out and get it actually. It's yellow. In the book it says "conjures up the atmosphere of an Arabian bazaar".
Amy Goodness.

They smile at one another again

Lawrence Oh, Amy, by the way. Did you answer the 'phone a few minutes ago?
Amy No.
Lawrence Oh. Only I've been expecting a call.
Amy Something urgent?
Lawrence Oh no.

Pause

Cissy Er . . . what time is . . . er . . . Arthur arriving?
Amy He's not coming.

Black-Out

The Lights come up on Amy, Lawrence and Cissy who sit in silence eating fried chicken out of take-away boxes

The telephone rings

Amy (*picking up the receiver*) Hello. . . . No, I'm afraid not. . . . Not yet. . . . Yes. . . . Yes of course I will. . . . Certainly. . . . Good-bye. (*She replaces the receiver*)

After a pause Lawrence clears his throat. Amy and Cissy look at him

Lawrence Ten o'clock. Rather late for anyone to telephone.
Amy (*agreeably*) Yes.

They are silent again

Lawrence (*in a businesslike tone*) I could, for example, prostrate myself at her feet.

He puts down his take-away box and goes and tidily lies face down on the floor in front of Amy. Neither she nor Cissy take any notice of him.

(*Quite loudly*) Where do you go, Amy? What do you do? What is happening? Tell me. Explain to me. (*Propping himself up on one elbow; bleakly conversational*) But it's patently not the sort of thing I would do. (*After a pause*) A month. First Cissy is summoned to come and live with us. Then Amy starts to go out. Sometimes in the daytime. Sometimes at night. We don't see her go. She's just not there. And I appear to have organized myself not to feel anything at all. With the exception of momentary intense irritation. Not at her, at myself. I dislike intensity of any kind. Before I met Amy I had, certainly, an intense and unwavering dislike of life generally. Which led in fact to my making a quite inept attempt to rid myself of it altogether. I was intensely surprised when she married me. So perfect a woman? Me? Since then I seem to have been able to seal off my intense belief that the world is not a good place and that life in it is a futile and ludicrous exercise. In this last month that belief has begun again to occur to me. I don't want to feel all that again. I don't want to! (*Pause*) I've managed to refrain from speculation about Arthur. He has not been to supper. Twice. I can cope with that information but doubt I could cope with anything more. To ask Amy where she

Act I

goes, what she does and what is happening might well lead me into areas of *Sturm und Drang* which I have neither the inclination nor the equipment to inhabit. Better not ask anything at all.

Lawrence remains on the floor

Cissy puts down her take-away box

Cissy (*thoughtfully*) I think probably on my knees, arms upraised ... hands clasped. (*She takes up this position beside Lawrence in front of Amy*) I wish I didn't always behave in such a way as to make this sort of image so suitable to me but I always do. I sometimes feel there was a possibility of my being quite a different kind of person but somehow or other I never pursued it. At any rate, the questions. Oh Amy, who? What? Where? Why? Oh Amy, why? (*She drops the pose*) I couldn't possibly. Absolutely not. Mainly because I've always been very much in awe of Amy. Even the first time they showed her to me lying in her Moses basket. Since then the central activity of my life has been loving and admiring Amy. She's the kindest, the most beautiful, the most generous woman I've ever known. (*After a pause*) I should never have said anything to Lawrence. I've got into the habit during my life of behaving in that impulsively agitated way. In this case the habit should most certainly not have been indulged. It's given me this uncomfortable feeling that Lawrence and I are two against one. Against? Oh dear. Better not ask anything at all.

Cissy and Lawrence get up and go back to their places and resume eating. They and Amy exchange smiles and make small, appreciative noises about the food

Amy (*looking straight out front*) They are not going to ask anything at all.

Black-Out

Lawrence and Cissy go out

Arthur comes on

Arthur Nothing at all?

The Lights come up on Arthur and Amy who clear all the furniture off stage as they talk. Throughout Amy never actually looks at Arthur

Amy No, really nothing. I spend a lot of time looking expectant and open and friendly but there are never any questions. Absolute silence.
Arthur They do say it speaks louder than words.
Amy What do you mean by that?
Arthur Silence. Maybe it asks questions louder than words too.
Amy I'm being insensitive. Is that what you're saying?
Arthur Think you are?
Amy Listen, Arthur, I've been married to Lawrence for over seven years. And I've known my sister all my life.
Arthur Yeah? So?
Amy It's only ... I've *been* attending to them all that time.
Arthur (*cheerfully*) Too true!

Amy I mean I've been sensitive to every feeling they had. You don't believe me but I have. I could always tell how they felt about anything. Just by looking at them. Just by the tone of their voices, for God's sake.
Arthur Why are you sounding so defiant about it all? I believe you. Anybody ever say you weren't probably one of the kindest, most considerate people going? Anybody ever say you didn't always put other people first, eh?
Amy (*helplessly*) I did!
Arthur I said. What? Get married to a bloke just to stop him trying to knock himself off?
Amy (*indignantly*) Not "just"! I loved him. Do. (*After a pause*) Love him.
Arthur Okay. Then you and him start up this art gallery for nuts from the looney bin to show their pictures in. Who'd you do that for, eh?
Amy The nuts . . . I mean, the mental patients. Well, and for Lawrence too.
Arthur Because he had to have something to do that made him feel like the whole number might be worthwhile?
Amy What whole number?
Arthur Life.
Amy Oh that.
Arthur So. What it adds up to is you are always doing whatever you think whoever they are want.
Amy (*depressed*) You make me sound like some kind of awful, semi-professional saint.
Arthur Nothing the matter with saints, mate. In their place. What're you getting in such a state about?
Amy Because I can't go on doing all that all the time anymore. I can't! Not now!
Arthur I know. Think they talk to each other about you? Cissy and Lawrence?
Amy Hard to tell. I didn't pick up any air of complicity when I came into the room this evening. Cissy had a kind of indefinable penumbra of guilt hovering about . . . but then she so often does.
Arthur And Lawrence?
Amy Well as a matter of fact he seems entirely calm.
Arthur You sound annoyed.
Amy Well, surprised. Disconcerted. I didn't expect to be taken quite so much in everybody's stride.
Arthur Would you say your main objective in all this is to unsettle Lawrence and Cissy?
Amy (*surprised*) Oh no. But one had reckoned on it as a side effect. After all, I've always been a very predictable and convenient person.
Arthur (*laughing*) Somehow that doesn't quite conjure you up.
Amy All right. Ordered. Harmonious. Sensible. Rational.
Arthur They may think you've gone mad.
Amy Oh. I hadn't thought of that. Of course. In which case they're "handling" me.
Arthur Like an unexploded bomb. Which, in a way, I suppose you are.
Amy (*cheerfully*) I suppose I am.

Act I

Arthur To pursue the metaphor, that would mean they're afraid of you. Of the possible explosion. Does that please you?
Amy (*indignantly*) No! (*After a pause*) Yes.
Arthur Yes.
Amy They take you in their stride too, you know. Nobody says Arthur who? Or who's Arthur?
Arthur I would be regarded as part of the bomb.
Amy Yes of course. When you think about it, the whole thing must be being quite difficult for them.
Arthur When you do, yes.
Amy Is that an accusation?
Arthur (*mildly*) No.

He puts a low footstool in the middle of the floor which is now empty except for the telephone, also on the floor

Amy (*getting up on the stool*) I don't see how we can go on living together in silence, all of us.
Arthur Perhaps you could initiate conversations about more or less anything. That way they might get around to asking the questions. (*After a pause*) If that's what you want.

Amy remains silent

Is that what you want?
Amy (*troubled*) I don't know.

Arthur takes the telephone and goes out

The Lights change to give the effect of bright sunlight

Cissy comes on carrying a sewing-box and kneels beside the stool. She begins pinning up the hem of Amy's dress

Amy It's awfully sweet of you, Cissy.
Cissy I'm not very good at it. Does that seem the right length?
Amy Perfect.

They are silent

Amy It's nice out here.
Cissy Yes, lovely.
Amy The sun's quite hot.
Cissy Summer at last.

They are silent again

Amy (*looking round*) The garden's getting awfully wild.
Cissy Lawrence did mention getting someone in to cut things down a bit.
Amy Oh no, he mustn't do that. I like doing it all myself.
Cissy (*looking up*) Yes but . . . (*She stops*)
Amy Yes but I'm not doing it at all?
Cissy (*swiftly*) I think it looks rather nice like this as a matter of fact.

More silence

Amy I had a rather peculiar fantasy this morning. Do you know that place you get into that isn't sleep but isn't being awake?
Cissy (*cautiously*) Yes . . .
Amy I had this idea that I was a boa constrictor with a half-dead donkey stuck down my throat.

Cissy freezes abolutely for a moment

Cissy (*desperately bright*) Oh yes? (*She resumes pinning the dress*)
Amy Yes. I'd crushed all its bones but it was still making a noise. Not a donkey noise. More like a baby. Whimpering. And I did have this quite strong feeling that it was, in an odd sort of way, my child. The word progeny. I seem to remember that. My progeny. The difficulty was I couldn't either swallow it down or vomit it up.
Cissy (*very upset*) Oh Amy! Just because you and Lawrence couldn't . . . I mean haven't . . . (*She stops*)
Amy (*interested*) What?
Cissy Well, I mean children . . . (*She falters with embarrassment*) I'm sorry.
Amy (*thoughtfully*) Oh I see.

More silence

Cissy (*reviving the social tone with effort*) What a terrible dream to have. Terrible.
Amy Well, it wasn't really like a dream. It seemed more sad than anything else. (*After a pause*) The place where I was . . . well where we were . . . was sad too. It was the bank of a river but there wasn't any water. Just cracked, dried up mud. And sand. Grey sand all around for as far as you could see.

Another silence

Cissy (*suddenly*) Like the moon.
Amy The moon?
Cissy (*slightly embarrassed*) I saw some pictures once in a magazine.
Amy (*thoughtfully*) The moon. A boa constrictor on the moon.

There is silence again

Cissy (*clearing her throat*) I've never cared much for the moon.
Amy (*with interest*) How do you mean?
Cissy (*busies herself with the dress*) I don't know. I don't know why I said that. It's silly really. It just seems too far away. Wrapped up in itself. There. I think that's finished. (*She sits back on her heels, assessing the hem*)
Amy Wrapped up in itself?
Cissy (*almost offhand*) It makes me feel left out.
Amy (*puzzled*) I don't understand that.
Cissy (*vaguely*) Well you know. I mean there you are on the earth wherever you happen to be. On a street or in a field or looking out of the window. Anyway, looking up. (*She looks up at Amy*) And there's the moon in the sky looking all . . . I said it was silly . . . oh I don't know.

Act I

Looking terribly calm and . . . well yes . . . mysterious. Secrets. (*Briskly*) I wonder if that is the right length.

Amy (*sitting on the stool*) Cissy, do you want to ask me anything?

Cissy (*getting up quickly*) No. No, I don't. I can't think what you mean. I must just pick some mint for the new potatoes.

Amy Not even why I asked you to come and live with us?

Cissy (*firmly*) No. I'm very grateful, that's all. Very, very grateful. The cooking . . . yes, that did baffle me. Does. But I expect you wanted me to have a creative outlet. We're having chops for lunch again. I seem to have got the hang of grilling chops though promise you'll say the moment they begin to pall. It's a whole new world to me, you see, and I . . .

Amy Or why Lawrence sleeps in the study?

Cissy Oh, Amy! The question couldn't possibly enter my mind. Not possibly. I would never . . . Insomnia I thought. Lawrence overtired. Insomnia. Not wanting to disturb you during the night he . . . Oh, Amy, it is none of my business! How can you ask such a . . . Marriage is inscrutable to me . . . Well of course I'm not a . . . practitioner. But nor am I a . . . a voyeur!

Amy (*distressed; getting up*) Oh, Cissy, I didn't think you were. I'm sorry. Forgive me. I didn't mean to . . .

Cissy (*calmly*) Not at all, of course you didn't. That was just me flying off the handle the way I do. I wish I didn't do that.

Amy You've always been very sensitive, Cissy. Highly strung. Sit down for a minute.

Affectionately she sits Cissy on the stool and sits on the ground beside her

Cissy (*gratefully*) Father used to say that. Highly strung. I liked it. It seemed . . . I mean I felt I might be like a harp or something. You know . . . as if even a breeze touching it would make it sound. (*She gives an embarrassed laugh*) Silly.

Amy No. Nice. (*After a pause*) Nice.

Cissy Anyway, I suppose it would be voyeuse, wouldn't it? For a woman I mean. How awful. Can't you just see her, Amy . . . all wrinkled and peering. (*Thoughtfully*) Now why does that seem so much worse than a man? Like the way people say "there is nothing worse than a drunken woman" and one can't help agreeing somehow. Oh dear, I'm afraid I'm just not feminist material.

Amy (*laughing*) Oh, Cissy.

They sit peacefully for a moment, enjoying the sunlight

Do you think Lawrence thinks Arthur is my lover?

Cissy Amy!

Amy Well, he must talk to you, doesn't he?

Cissy No, no, no, he doesn't! He wouldn't!

Amy (*getting up*) Shall I tell you how I met Arthur, Cissy? I'd like to tell you.

Cissy (*getting up*) Amy, I don't want to hear.

Amy It was that night at the end of April when it snowed, do you remember? I couldn't sleep so I decided to go out for a walk. Just a sudden impulse and I . . .

Cissy interrupts her and they both speak at once not listening to each other and gradually increasing in volume until they are almost shouting by the end of the speeches

Amy *(together)* . . . went out the front door and there he was taking photographs of our house. At first I was frightened but then we started to talk. It was amazing because everything was changed. Everything! I could see that nothing would ever be the same!

Cissy *(together)* I don't want to listen, Amy! I don't want to! As far as I'm concerned you and Lawrence are simply a perfect couple and I'm quite convinced that all this—which I don't understand and don't want to—is a passing phase and absolutely none of my business!

They stop, look at each other and suddenly both laugh

Cissy How awful! How awful of us!
Amy What will the neighbours think?
Cissy Bellowing at each other! They'd think we were mad.
Amy Or drunk and disorderly.
Cissy Disturbing the peace. (*She stops laughing*) You were, Amy.
Amy What?
Cissy Disturbing the peace.
Amy Yours do you mean?
Cissy Well, yes. But Lawrence's too it would be.
Amy Because you'd tell him whatever I . . .
Cissy I wouldn't tell him. But he would know that I knew.
Amy Why wouldn't you?
Cissy Lawrence and I don't have that kind of conversation, Amy. How could we? (*Angrily*) And how could you! Boa constrictors . . . half-dead donkeys. It's wrong to tell things like that. Forget them, you must forget them! We don't need to know!
Amy Oh, Cissy, they're interesting.
Cissy (*flatly*) No they're not. They're dangerous. It's hard enough keeping things more or less . . . (*She stops*)
Amy (*after a pause, gently*) What do you mean?
Cissy Amy, all these years I've been coming here to Sunday lunch and for my week in June. You and Lawrence . . . everything about you. Your life, this house, the work you both do. Imagine starting such a wonderful organization as Minds Unlimited together! All those poor, poor people you've helped. You're famous. Oh I know you don't care about that. You and Lawrence aren't interested in anything so . . . so frivolous. But I was proud. I am! I am proud! To belong in a way . . . well, to be attached. And now you . . .

Lawrence comes on, interrupting Cissy

Act I

Lawrence Oh, here you are. I've had a rather urgent telephone call, Amy.
Amy Oh yes?
Lawrence From Gabriel. He's just flown in from Brussels. He says his secretary's been trying to get through to me for days. Which seems odd. (*Swiftly*) But of no importance. What Gabriel says is that he's afraid he's about to have a nervous breakdown and he wants to come and stay here.
Amy A nervous breakdown? But he's a psychiatrist.
Lawrence I don't think that makes him exempt.
Amy I told him he was mad to go and live in Brussels. But why does he want to have it here?
Lawrence He doesn't. He thinks being with friends might stave it off.
Amy How very odd.
Lawrence (*after a brief pause*) Anyway I've told him to come to supper tonight to talk it over.
Cissy Supper? Oh dear.
Amy Never mind, Cissy. I'll cook supper.
Cissy Thank you, Amy. That's very kind.
Amy (*kisses her*) And I'm sorry, Cissy. Forgive me. Well, I must be off.
Cissy (*distressed*) But . . . but . . . what about your lunch?
Amy (*making her way out*) I'll have some there.
Lawrence (*loudly*) Where?

Amy stops and turns to look at him. There is a brief pause while they look at each other. She takes a step forward and goes to speak

(*Rapidly*) You wouldn't object to Gabriel staying here for a bit?
Amy (*after a brief pause*) No. No, of course not.

Amy goes out

Cissy and Lawrence avoid looking at each other

Cissy (*starting to go out. Erratically*) I'll . . . er . . . I should probably just . . . the lunch . . .
Lawrence Cissy . . .
Cissy (*fluently*) Chops, new potatoes and frozen peas. Plain sailing, I hope.
Lawrence Sorry for what? Amy said she was sorry.
Cissy Ah. Yes. Well. Er . . . for teasing me! She's always done it. Since we were children. Does she tease you, Lawrence? (*Quickly*) No, I'm sure she doesn't. What a ridiculous question. And butterscotch whip for pudding. Out of a packet, I'm afraid, but I think some compromises are really unavoidable don't you?
Lawrence (*going up very close to her; urgently*) Compromises? Yes, you're right, Cissy. That's true. What would you advise me to . . .
Cissy (*backing away*) Compromises about the cooking. Me and the cooking. Advise, Lawrence? I wouldn't. How could I? I wouldn't presume. Apart from which I'm not at all sure I follow you. If you'll excuse me I think I'll just go and run some cold water over my wrists.

Cissy runs out

Lawrence gazes after her

Lawrence (*sighing*) Yes. (*Sighing again*) Yes.

He walks aimlessly about for a moment or two, kicks a twig or something similar out of his path and then begins to wander off. As he walks he sings dreamily and sadly under his breath

> (*singing*) "My name is Captain Spalding, the African explorer, hello I must be going, good-bye, good-bye, good-bye . . ."

Lawrence goes out passing Arthur who is coming on and walking upstage of him in the opposite direction. Arthur picks up the stool and goes out

Amy comes on carrying a tray with coffee and brandy on it. Arthur comes on with a coffee table which he puts down and Amy places the tray on the table. During the next scene they bring on four garden chairs and, perhaps, a potted plant while continuing to speak

The Light changes to outdoor evening light

Arthur After dinner coffee on the terrace is it?
Amy Yes. And brandy.
Arthur All been sitting round the supper table breaking bread together, eh?
Amy Well . . . breaking blanquette de veau together, actually.
Arthur (*as if reciting*) Amy is a marvellous cook.
Amy (*factually*) Yes.
Arthur Pleasant evening?
Amy Yes and no. So far so good, I'd say.
Arthur (*amiably*) Well . . . so far, so far.

Gabriel comes strolling on

Gabriel (*sniffing the air*) Glorious. Wisteria?
Amy Night-blooming stock.

Gabriel walks downstage and prepares to sit down on nothing. Arthur puts a chair under him

Arthur What's he really here for?
Amy Well, I think Lawrence must have s.o.s.'d him.
Arthur To come and have a look at you? See what you're up to?
Amy That's my guess. Coffee, Gabriel?
Gabriel Thank you. Just black.

She takes him a cup of coffee

Amy He's Lawrence's best friend . . . well, only friend, really. It's difficult for Lawrence to believe people like him because he doesn't really like himself. He and Gabriel went to prep school, Winchester and Cambridge together. And brandy, Gabriel?
Gabriel Please.

Amy goes and pours him a glass and takes it to him

Act I

Amy Gabriel always behaves as if he'd invented Lawrence, which I find quite maddening.
Gabriel (*taking the glass*) Thank you.

She smiles at him and goes back to the chair

Amy (*sitting down*) It's Lawrence's fault. He lets Gabriel bully him. Though, to be fair, Gabriel always worked very hard at convincing Lawrence that it was all right to stay alive. I thought he'd be called in to pronounce on the situation. Like the Pope. Nervous breakdown, my foot. He wouldn't know how to break down. He's always absolutely sure about absolutely everything.
Gabriel You're very quiet.
Arthur (*laughing*) Toodloo.

Arthur goes out

Amy Just a bit tired. I didn't sleep much last night.
Gabriel Oh really? Why not?
Amy (*very brightly*) Because I'd been snorting cocaine in a flat in Leicester Square.
Gabriel (*appalled*) Amy!
Amy A joke. You certainly don't behave like someone having a breakdown. You ate a huge supper and you're just as bossy as ever.
Gabriel I didn't say I was having one. I said I was afraid I might be going to.
Amy (*sceptically*) What makes you think that?
Gabriel (*loftily*) My own observations. It is my profession.
Amy You mean you have symptoms?
Gabriel (*repressively*) Yes.
Amy Well, what are they? Hallucinations? Persecution fantasies?
Gabriel I cry.
Amy Cry? You?
Gabriel Yes, me. Why is that so unthinkable? It happens suddenly and without any warning. That's why I'm taking some time off. I can't weep in front of my patients.
Amy (*laughing*) No, I suppose not. I don't know, though. It might do them good to see you falling to pieces, those trendy Common Market types of yours. It might even cure them. The sight of the majestic Doctor Foster seized by sobs.
Gabriel Really, Amy, your ignorance about the therapeutic relationship is total.
Amy Would you be offended if I said thank God? More coffee?
Gabriel (*tidily*) Not at all. And yes, please.
Amy Do you cry about something? Something particular?
Gabriel (*with simple pomposity*) I think probably about everything.
Amy Oh, Gabriel how grand! I'll come and be your patient if you promise to cry a lot of the time.
Gabriel You know, for a woman who's quite warm and compassionate, you're really rather callous in some ways.

Amy (*interestedly*) Am I? (*Looking back towards the house*) Where are the others?
Gabriel Your sister insisted on clearing the table. Stacking and rinsing, she said. Lawrence tried and failed to stop her and then joined her.
Amy Cissy insisted. It sounds right but it's not a thing she often does. Insist.
Gabriel I rather thought she might be a touch tipsy.
Amy (*pleased*) I hope so. I think she's enjoying herself.
Gabriel And Lawrence?
Amy And Lawrence what?
Gabriel Is he enjoying himself? Why was he so bad tempered at supper?
Amy (*slightly irritated*) I don't know. How should I know? (*To herself*) Oh God, sometimes I really feel so . . .
Gabriel Yes? You feel so what?
Amy (*contemptuously*) Really, Gabriel, if you've been asked to come and spy on me, you're being very obvious about it.
Gabriel (*astonished*) Spy on you, Amy? What on earth do you mean? What for?
Amy Oh, come on, Gabriel. All this melodrama. Urgent telephone calls from abroad. And you of all people cracking up. It's so silly. I would have thought you two could think up something better than that.
Gabriel Think up? What are you talking about?
Amy And as for you weeping. I might have believed hallucinations.
Gabriel Amy you astonish me.

Lawrence comes in followed a little way behind by Cissy

Lawrence Amy astonishes everyone.
Amy Do I astonish you, Cissy?
Cissy (*promptly*) No, of course not, Amy, certainly not. Oh dear.

There is a silence

(*Rather precipitantly*) Though of course when you come to think of it all human beings are astonishing. The digestive system, the brain, the heart . . . all quite amazing really. Photosynthesis . . . though of course that's plants. What a wonderful supper, Amy. Didn't you think so, Doctor Foster?
Gabriel Very good. Excellent.
Cissy Amy is a marvellous cook. I've made a decision not to be cast down by that but inspired.
Amy (*laughing*) Oh good. Brandy, Cissy? Coffee?
Cissy Oh yes, thank you, Amy. Lovely.

Amy takes a brandy and cup of coffee to Cissy

Amy Just brandy for you, Lawrence?
Lawrence Yes. Quite a lot, please.
Cissy No coffee? (*Pleased*) You do have insomnia.

Amy hands Lawrence a glass of brandy

Lawrence (*surprised*) No. I just don't like coffee. But if I drink enough brandy I may sing something a little later.

Act I

Gabriel God preserve us.
Amy Really, Lawrence? Would you? Now, you astonish me.
Lawrence (*in a friendly tone*) Counter-astonishment tactics, you see. That could be the solution.
Gabriel (*testily*) Solution? Solution to what? What's that supposed to mean?
Lawrence (*with sudden aggressive exasperation*) Supposed to mean? Have I ever struck you as the kind of person who would know what things are supposed to mean? Have I ever laid any claim whatsoever to that kind of facility?
Gabriel (*rather unpleasantly*) Perhaps a song would be better than this heavy rhetoric.
Amy Gabriel!
Gabriel (*blandly*) Sorry.
Lawrence (*depressed*) No. My fault. (*He sits down heavily*) Oh God.

There is an awkward silence

Cissy (*trying to fill the breach; chattily*) I saw the most extraordinary old tramp yesterday. Skulking along beside the garden wall . . . Amy do you remember that crazy old woman we used to see down at the railway station when we were children?
Amy (*offhand*) Oh yes.
Cissy Well, this one was exactly like her! It was quite uncanny . . . she even limped just the same way. (*To Gabriel*) We were terrified of her but absolutely fascinated too. Remember, Amy? We pretended to father that we'd become train spotters so we'd have an excuse to go down to the station and look for her.
Amy We were train spotters. We had little notebooks.
Lawrence I was a train spotter once, too.
Cissy Were you, Lawrence? How nice!
Lawrence (*puzzledly*) Nice?
Cissy (*abashedly*) Well, I . . . I mean . . . (*Taking a breath*) That's three I've thought of today.
Lawrence Three what?
Cissy I was just thinking . . . I mean about that old woman. Why should a crazy woman tramp seem so much worse than a crazy man one? The other two were drunkards and voyeurs. Women ones being worse. It seems a disloyal thing to think. For me, I mean, as a woman.
Gabriel Not at all. It's a universally held response. The only implication is that women are intrinsically better than men. Therefore the more shocking to see them fall.
Cissy I hadn't thought of that. So it's really a sort of compliment.
Amy It isn't at all. Quite the opposite. The universal expectation is that women are supposed to be virtuous. It's impertinent of them to be vicious. That's what shocks people. They're behaving out of character. Being unsuitable.
Gabriel Rubbish.
Lawrence (*urgently to Amy*) Vicious, Amy? *Vicious?*

There is another awkward pause

Cissy (*rushing in*) This old woman we used to see . . . she talked all the time. Muttered and waved her stick about. She was always saying, "Think you're so clever, don't you! Think you're so clever." I used to wonder if it would cheer her up at all if I told her I didn't. I wouldn't have dared of course. She always seemed so angry.
Gabriel What was the one today saying?
Cissy (*startled*) Oh, I don't know. I was watching from behind the window. (*After a pause*) She made me feel rather hopeless as a matter of fact.
Gabriel Hopeless?
Cissy Well, yes. There are some things you see. Or people. And you think, oh God if that's what it's about . . . life, I mean. You know. Then there's not really much point in it at all. There are quite a number of things one sees that makes one feel like that. (*After a pause*) Well, there are for me. (*She is slightly embarrassed*) I seem to be talking a great deal tonight. I do beg everybody's pardon.
Gabriel No need whatsoever. Why apologize?
Amy (*smiling at Cissy*) Habit.
Lawrence (*suddenly*) Hopeless.

They all look at him

Hopeless is a man. Bound to be. A bundle of rags under Waterloo Bridge . . . the face behind the bars in the condemned cell. Definitely male. Yes. (*After a pause*) Whereas hope . . . has to be female. Isn't that odd but I'm sure I'm right. I tend to see hope as a rather plain but really very nice woman of indeterminate age sidling into the room dressed in a pink tutu that's too small for her. And wearing one of those red clown noses to show that she knows the whole thing is something of a joke. That's hope.
Gabriel (*after a pause*) Are you drunk, Lawrence?
Lawrence No. That was my aim but I've only drunk myself into a headache. I think I'll go to bed.
Amy (*sadly*) No singing.
Lawrence No. Perhaps it isn't in me to astonish. Perhaps that's female too. (*He looks straight at Amy. After a pause*) Or might it astonish you, Amy, to know that I've resigned from the Board.
Amy (*holding his gaze*) Yes.
Gabriel You're not serious, Lawrence!
Lawrence Odd you should say that. It's something I've found myself saying rather a lot to myself lately. "You're not serious, Lawrence." And by and large that does seem to be true. I did think, you see, that I cared passionately about Minds Unlimited but I find I don't. It all seems rather ludicrous.
Gabriel (*impatiently*) Oh, come come, Lawrence. You can't call it ludicrous. The work you two do is extremely ennabling.
Lawrence Is that what it is? Yes, I suppose it is.

Act I

Gabriel (*becoming angry*) You know perfectly well that it is. Why are you being so boring and bizarre?
Lawrence (*angrily*) All right, not ludicrous. Meaningless.
Gabriel Really, Lawrence, you're intolerable. That's such an arrogant thing to say.
Lawrence That I feel meaningless? Would you call that arrogant?
Gabriel Your feelings are a great deal less important than the work. Minds Unlimited is a unique organization and you know it.
Amy It's only unique because all the pictures we exhibit in the gallery are by loonies.
Gabriel Tasteless, Amy. (*Turning to Lawrence*) Unique because you are providing a very particular kind of patronage. For example, how many is it of your . . . exhibitors that have gone on to become proper artists?
Amy Twenty-four in five years. What do you mean by proper?
Gabriel Oh come along, Amy. Really, you two are being very exasperating this evening. Twenty-four. And dozens more of them being given a crucial sense of fulfilment. It's self-indulgent and tedious of you to be doing all this, Lawrence.
Lawrence Well, tedious is what I'm finding it. The whole thing.
Amy Is that true, Lawrence?
Lawrence Oh yes. And meaningless. And ludicrous too, I'm afraid.
Gabriel Nonsense. And besides how do you propose to live?
Lawrence I don't know. All I know is what I feel. Now that Amy's out of it, you see . . .

Cissy is becoming increasingly upset

Gabriel No, I don't see. What do you mean "out of it"?
Cissy (*leaping up*) Don't Lawrence, don't! She'll come back to it, won't you, Amy? She will, Lawrence, I promise! You mustn't . . . both of you . . . it's wrong! Letting things fall apart . . . be lost. It can all go on again just the same. It will! It will! Exactly the same!
Amy Don't cry, Cissy.
Cissy I tried to tell you this morning but you wouldn't listen. You and Lawrence . . . this place . . . it's like an island in the middle of all the . . . oh you know what I mean. This was safe. And now both of you . . . everything you say sounds so . . . I can't bear it. I'm sorry, I'm terribly sorry, I'm being a fool.
Amy (*going to her*) Cissy, don't . . .
Cissy (*fiercely*) Leave me alone, Amy! (*Immediately shocked at herself*) Oh forgive me . . . I shouldn't have . . . Oh God I . . .

She runs out crying

Amy (*starting to go after her*) Cissy, wait!
Gabriel Get out of the way, Amy. I'll look after her.

Gabriel goes out
Amy stands helpless for a moment

Amy (*turning to Lawrence*) But what did I do?

Lawrence shrugs

You think I was being cruel to her?
Lawrence I have no idea, Amy.
Amy Oh Lawrence, don't.
Lawrence No truly, Amy, I have no idea about anything. I am absolutely without ideas. I'm going for a walk.

He starts to go out

Amy (*following him*) Lawrence!

Lawrence turns

Couldn't we talk?
Lawrence (*after a brief pause*) No.

He goes out

Amy Damn! Damn! Damn! I feel like a criminal!

Arthur comes on. Amy avoids looking at him while they speak to each other

Arthur Oh yeah? Why's that?
Amy Bloody Gabriel! Like some kind of avenging Nanny. Me! My fault! It's all my fault!
Arthur All what?
Amy Tonight. Cissy. Lawrence.
Arthur Yeah, well. Looks like Question Time's come around.
Amy What do you mean? Nobody asked me anything.
Arthur (*laughing*) How did you see it, Amy, eh? Hands up take your turn? The Chair will now accept questions from the Floor? Doesn't usually work like that. Sirens and bells, more. Flocks of birds flying out of the trees. Fountains of water in the street. People shouting . . . dogs barking . . . somebody singing somewhere. Feet running past in the dark. (*After a pause*) Know what I mean?
Amy (*subdued and troubled*) No. I don't understand.
Arthur Who's talking about understanding? Things are going on, Amy. (*After a pause*) Did you know that every second somewhere in the world a peacock mounts a peahen?
Amy (*surprised*) Surely not.
Arthur (*amiably*) Maybe not. Well, here's a question for you. Can you remember why you started all this? How it began?
Amy Certainly. Meeting you.
Arthur Must have been something before that. Otherwise you wouldn't have listened to me at all that night. You would have bolted.
Amy Yes I would. I nearly did . . . (*After a pause*) Before. Well, I'd been having a lot of odd feelings. Things I'd never felt before. I felt like a stranger to myself a lot of the time. I mean I knew what I was doing but I couldn't always tell why I was doing it. Simple things like setting the table or reading a book. Everything got to feeling sort of arbitrary and random. I used to feel anticipation and apprehension both at the same

Act I

time. I'd walk around the house touching things. Sometimes I'd hop up and down on one foot or . . . or stretch my arms out as far as I could. I couldn't keep still. I also had this very profound conviction that I was a cheat. Everything I did . . . everything I'd ever done . . . a cheat.

Arthur This been going on for long all this?

Amy Oh weeks. And there wasn't anybody I could . . . No, wait. I tried to talk to Gabriel about it. *(After a pause; with surprise)* How odd! That was the same night I met you! I'd forgotten all about that conversation with Gabriel. He'd come over from Brussels for the Easter weekend. That's right . . . he'd come to supper that night too! We had a row!

Arthur picks up the tray and coffee table and starts to go out with them

Arthur *(as he goes)* Was Lawrence there?

He goes out

Amy No, he wasn't. Where was he? Oh yes . . . another bloody Board Meeting. *(After a pause)* And the snow! Of course!

Arthur comes on carrying Amy's coat into which he helps her. He goes out

The Lights change to blue-white and give the effect of snow falling

Amy Snow in April!

Gabriel comes on buttoning up his overcoat

Gabriel I don't know why you sound so delighted about it. I think it's an outrage.

Amy *(laughing)* An outrage. Well, I suppose. Nature flying in the face of Nature. But so beautiful, Gabriel. Look at the apple tree. You can't tell the difference between the snow and the blossom. You must admit it's very beautiful.

Gabriel Certainly. And cold. Now we've seen it why don't we go back in.

Amy Not yet. Not yet.

Gabriel Because you don't want to continue that conversation?

Amy What?

Gabriel Isn't that why you came tearing out here? Running away?

Amy No it wasn't. I wanted to see the snow. Anyway why should I run away from a conversation I'd started myself?

Gabriel It's what ninety-nine per cent of my patients do ninety-nine per cent of the time.

Amy I'm not your patient.

Gabriel No, thank God. But you sound as if perhaps you ought to be somebody's.

Amy *(interestedly)* Are you saying I'm a nutter?

Gabriel Oh Amy, this *faux naif* thing you do is so tiresome. My patients are not "nutters". They are, in the main, confused and unhappy.

Amy I'm not unhappy. I feel quite . . . I don't know. It's a sort of combination of very peaceful and very agitated. *(Walking away from him)* I don't know. I don't know.

Gabriel You said you had to talk to me and now all you can do is . . .

(*After a pause*) You said "cheat". Amy, is all this about you and Lawrence? Are you trying to tell me . . .
Amy Oh for God's sake, Gabriel!
Gabriel You told me you felt like a cheat.
Amy To myself! Myself! Does everything always have to be about me and Lawrence? I am faithful as the day is long if that's what you're getting at.
Gabriel I'm very glad to hear it.
Amy I'm sure you are. Who I want to talk about is me . . . as me.
Gabriel In that case let us take you as you inside.
Amy I can't talk in there. Shall we go for a walk?
Gabriel No. But if you insist on staying outside we will walk up and down the terrace. It's too cold for standing about.
Amy All right.

Gabriel takes her arm and they walk

Gabriel Now. Why do you feel like a cheat?
Amy I don't know.
Gabriel You've said "I don't know" at least eleven times in the last fifteen minutes. What do you know?
Amy (*stopping*) If you'd just listen for a minute.
Gabriel (*firmly*) Keep walking, Amy. Try and imagine you're on shipboard.
Amy A stroll on deck with the captain. How posh.
Gabriel Will you get on, Amy?
Amy I am, I am. Listen. Lately I've been getting these awful sudden feelings about . . . don't say naive again . . . this is true. Sort of overwhelming feelings about things like injustice and cruelty and suffering.
Gabriel You sound like any other good *Guardian* reader.
Amy (*irritated*) I don't read the *Guardian*! I hate reading newspapers. I mean I know all those names. Like Ethiopia and the Lebanon and Zaire . . . but I have no idea at all what's going on in them. Who's on what side or what it means.
Gabriel You sound rather proud of all this, Amy.
Amy Oh God, do I? (*She stops*) I wonder if I am.
Gabriel (*pulling her on*) At any rate, these feelings.
Amy Well, they're tied up with a sort of continuous odd sensation that there's something . . . something going on. I mean for me. I can nearly hear it, nearly see it, if you know what I mean, but I can't get hold of it. It makes me feel infuriated. And scared. And optimistic.
Gabriel You have a way of making things seem much too complicated, Amy. My guess is that it's a simple surplus of creative energy.
Amy Ah. You think I should enrol in evening classes. Short story writing or poetry. Or flower arranging you might consider more my line.
Gabriel I wish you wouldn't tell me what I'm going to say in that irritating way. Now, it's my opinion that advice is almost invariably a bad thing but here is some. You won't take it anyway.
Amy I might.

Act I

Gabriel I doubt it. You don't respect me much and you suffer from morbid egotism. However. I've always been rather surprised that you were politically so . . . comatose. I think you should espouse some political cause.
Amy Any cause at all?
Gabriel Anything that engages your affect . . . your passion. The way Minds Unlimited did when you started it. Lawrence and the Board really run it now. You're a beginner of things, Amy. Find a cause. Perhaps something to do with children.
Amy Why do you say that?
Gabriel No need to be edgy. Some of these feelings of yours are bound to come from your not having had children. Minds Unlimited itself, for example. In a way you provide a mothering facility for those mental patients. Helping them to grow up.
Amy What a very whimsical metaphor. You sound like a vicar.
Gabriel I would have made an excellent vicar. By the way, I've never known, is it you or Lawrence who's infertile?
Amy We asked them not to tell us at the clinic. We thought it might get in the way. I mean between us. Knowing.

The snow effect stops

Gabriel Somehow that's very typical of you and Lawrence.
Amy (*sadly*) It's stopped snowing.
Gabriel Good. Let's go in. (*Starting to move*) And if you can't find a suitable cause you might stand for Parliament.
Amy Gabriel! You're laughing at me!
Gabriel Not in the least. I've no doubt at all you could be elected. You're an exceedingly powerful person.
Amy And a morbid egotist.
Gabriel They often go together. Come along in, Amy.
Amy Session's over, Amy. Ready steady go, Amy. Run along and find something to begin, Amy. Well I don't want a political cause, thanks very much! None of them are ever clear cut. As soon as you get involved in any political anything, some of what you do is bound to be phoney.
Gabriel (*angrily*) Clear cut! What makes you think that anything under the sun is clear cut. Dear God, are you actually saying that your integrity is more important than injustice and suffering and all those large things you've been so sensitively brooding on? Some of what all of us do all the time is phoney. We are fallen creatures every one. That is as you might say the deal. However the task, the task, Amy, would seem to be to make some kind of attempt to save ourselves and when possible each other. Your fastidious sensibilities are appallingly self-indulgent and absolutely irrelevant. Is the entire world to revolve around your *feelings*?
Amy Don't bloody patronize me, Gabriel!
Gabriel I wouldn't dream of such a thing. And now I am going in. I am frozen to the marrow. And bored. And I want some brandy. (*As he goes*) Shall I pour you some?

Amy (*rudely*) Yes. Lots.

Gabriel goes out

Amy walks back to where she was standing before Gabriel came in. Arthur comes on with the tray and table and puts them down. He takes the coat from Amy

The Lights change to general centre stage

Gabriel (*off*) Amy?
Amy (*shouting angrily*) I said, yes!

Gabriel comes in, he is without his coat

Gabriel You said yes what? Why are you shouting?
Arthur Get into the now, Amy. Go with the flow, buddy.

Arthur goes out

Amy Sorry, Gabriel, nothing. I was thinking about something else.
Gabriel Where's Lawrence?
Amy Gone for a walk.
Gabriel Cissy is getting herself some hot milk and two aspirins. We had a little talk. She seems quite calm now.

Cissy screams off stage

Gabriel My God!
Amy Cissy!
Zoe (*off*) Let go of me, you silly old twat! Let go!

Zoe comes on. She is nineteen and wearing lots of make-up and a luxuriant wig and dressed in a flashy, very sexy way

Cissy, who is very upset, rushes on after her wearing a dressing-gown

All right. Where is he?
Cissy I couldn't stop her! I was putting the milk bottles out. She was there on the front step. She . . .
Zoe What have you done with him? I know he's here.
Gabriel Who? What do you want?
Cissy She nearly knocked me down.
Zoe Arthur. I want Arthur.
Cissy Arthur!
Zoe Where is he?
Amy Zoe. It's you!

Lawrence has come on. He stands at the edge of the stage, unseen by the others, watching the scene

Zoe What's the matter, Amy? Didn't you recognize me?
Amy No I didn't. You look so . . .
Zoe Surprised, eh? Good. Now where's Arthur?
Gabriel Amy, who is this?
Zoe I'm Arthur's sister that's who I bloody am and I bloody want him. I know he's here.
Amy He isn't, Zoe, honestly. You know he doesn't come here.

Act I

Zoe Don't fucking well lie to me, Amy.
Gabriel Look here! We don't have to . . .
Cissy She isn't lying. (*Getting in front of Amy and speaking earnestly*) Arthur isn't here. Not here. Your brother—Not—Here.
Zoe Piss off, you. What do you think I am? Fucking blind? Course he's here. I followed him. I saw him go in through that door in the wall. I've been waiting, haven't I? He didn't leave. I would've seen him.

Arthur comes on and stands in the darkness at the edge of the stage

Arthur Think you're so clever, don't you!
Gabriel Who's that?

Arthur comes into the light. He is dressed the same as Amy was at the beginning of the play in the woollen hat; bulky ragged army coat; dirty sneakers; steel-rimmed glasses and wild, grey wig. He also carries the stick and bulging plastic bag. Zoe, Gabriel, Amy, Cissy and Lawrence stand and stare at him

Arthur (*waving the stick*) Stupid, silly sods the lot of you. Think I don't know? Eh?
Cissy It's her!
Amy (*clutching Cissy*) Cissy! Oh, Cissy, save me!
Arthur (*going over to Zoe*) What you doin' here, Zoe?
Zoe Sorry, Art, did I do wrong?
Arthur And what you dolled up like that for?
Zoe But Art . . .
Amy Oh Arthur, it's you!
Arthur (*taking off the wig and hat*) That's right. Off you go then, Zoe. Get moving.
Zoe (*cheerfully*) Righto. Tada, all.

Zoe goes out

Arthur (*to Amy*) You coming?
Amy Yes.

Amy and Arthur go out

Cissy Amy! Amy come back!

Cissy runs out after Amy and Arthur

Gabriel sinks down into the chair and a door slams offstage

Lawrence comes forward into the light. Cissy comes back on and sees him

Oh Lawrence, Amy's gone! She's gone!
Lawrence Well that's what she does, isn't it?
Cissy No, no, you don't understand. (*After a pause*) She asked me to save her.
Lawrence (*going to Gabriel*) Gabriel, what is it? Why are you crying?
Gabriel (*angrily weeping*) I don't know! I don't know!

BLACK-OUT

ACT II

Arthur's room stage right. It is very small with a door, a set of bunk beds against a wall, a small table with a typewriter on it, a bookshelf containing some books, a chair and a footlocker which is placed against the end of the lower bunk. Zoe's "tart" costume and some of the tramp costume are bundled up on the lower bunk

Arthur is sitting on a stool at the table. Amy stands, leaning against the bunk beds, watching him type

Arthur Who was that geezer . . . the one in the specs?

Amy (*surprised*) But you know who he is. I told you. (*After a pause*) Oh no of course . . . I didn't!

Arthur Eh? I'm not with you. (*He stops typing*)

Amy (*slightly embarrassed*) Oh, it's just that I'm always talking to you in my head when you're not there. It's odd, really. Tonight was the first time you actually were in my house and yet in a way you've been there the whole time.

Arthur (*without interest*) Oh yeah? Well, who is he?

Amy Gabriel Foster. He's a psychiatrist.

Arthur resumes typing

He goes in too?

Arthur Course. It all goes in. Everything just about. One of you go to him then?

Amy Go to . . .? Oh. Oh no. He's just a friend.

Arthur Is he married?

Amy He was. She died five years ago. Lena. She was one of the most awful people I've ever known. She was always saying things like "If you want my absolutely frank opinion" . . . which you didn't. And she didn't shave her legs.

Arthur (*laughing*) Eh?

Amy Well, I always thought she left them hairy like that just to upset people. I mean they looked so terrible. Some women have nice hairy legs and I can imagine that could be quite sexy but Lena's were just so aggressively awful they made you feel really depressed.

Arthur (*laughing*) Oh come on, Amy.

Amy No, I mean it. Cissy said tonight that some things you see make you feel hopeless. Well, Lena's legs would have made anybody feel absolutely desolate. She was always very contemptuous about women anyway. I think she didn't like being one. Perhaps that's why Gabriel married her. I've always thought he might be an undeclared homosexual.

Arthur Why'd you think that?

Act II

Amy Well . . . Him and Lawrence. He only really puts up with me at all because of Lawrence. Lawrence loves me and Gabriel loves Lawrence.
Arthur (*reprovingly*) You don't have to be a pouffta to love another bloke, you know.
Amy I didn't mean that. I've never thought they were lovers but I think that when they were young they loved each other better than anybody else. Gabriel always protected Lawrence, you see. I used to find myself feeling amazingly jealous of Gabriel years ago. Not now, though. I'm being boring.
Arthur No you're not. I can listen and type. I always like the way you ramble on. (*He stops typing, looks at her and grins*) The first couple of weeks I knew you you never hardly opened your mouth. Now look at you. Ramble, ramble.
Amy (*comfortably*) Well, I was afraid of you.
Arthur Yeah. (*They smile at each other*) Is it Cissy with an "s" or a "c"?
Amy "C".
Arthur What's it short for?
Amy It's short for sister.
Arthur Doesn't she have a name?
Amy Yes . . . Ann. But everybody's always called her Cissy.
Arthur Always? Anyway why not "s" then? "C" isn't short for sister.

Zoe comes on, wearing a djellabah. Her hair is cut very short like a boy's and she wears no make-up. She is carrying a tray with three mugs, a pot of honey and a sugar bowl on it

Zoe Tea?
Arthur Thanks, Zo.
Zoe You going to try honey in it, Amy?
Amy (*a little guiltily*) No thank you, Zoe. I really don't like the taste.
Zoe (*sighing*) If I could only convince you how bad sugar is for you . . . (*Handing the cup to Amy*) Arthur takes honey.
Arthur Only to keep you quiet, mate. I don't want the old Yin and Yang lecture seventy-seven times a day.
Zoe You amaze me, Arthur, you really do. Everything you take into your body is important.
Arthur Here we go. You can't control intake into the body any more than you can to the mind. You're taking in petrol fumes and chemicals and all sorts every time you breathe. Just like your mind takes in whatever there is floating around. You can't control it.
Zoe You can control some of it, Arthur, you can! (*After a brief pause she continues sadly*) I know you think I'm stupid.
Arthur (*surprised*) I don't. What a thing to say, Zo.
Zoe Sorry. I'm the one. It's the dressing up. It always makes me feel a bit peculiar after.
Arthur Funny thing me forgetting it was going to be both of us tonight.
Zoe Amy knew. That was really good, Amy. "Cissy, save me!" Gave me goosebumps.

Amy (*upset*) Zoe! I didn't know! I never expected Arthur to be dressed up like that. I wouldn't frighten Cissy on purpose. Never.

Zoe Sorry, Amy. I didn't mean to hurt your feelings or anything.

Arthur Hang on a sec. Never? (*Sorting through a stack of yellow paper on the table. He reads from one sheet*) "Told Cissy about the boa constrictor and the donkey this morning. She hated it." (*He grins at Amy*)

Amy (*slightly embarrassed*) That was only teasing. Cissy doesn't mind that. But I wouldn't pretend to her about something being dangerous. It would be so cruel. Cissy's very highly strung. It would be a vicious thing to . . . (*After a brief pause she continues somewhat aggressively*) I'm not a monster!

Arthur No need getting in a state, Amy. Nobody's calling you a monster.

Zoe (*warmly*) Course not. Look how you was so worried about her tonight we had to stop at the first 'phone box so you could call her and tell her you hadn't been kidnapped or something.

Arthur You talk to Lawrence too, by the way?

Amy Yes, I did.

Arthur Give him the same spiel?

Amy Yes. (*Reciting pompously*) I am doing part-time voluntary care work with ex-mental patients.

They all laugh

I wonder if he believed it. I wouldn't.

Zoe Oh I don't know, Amy. People like to know the reasons for things. Even if the reason sounds daft. Especially if they're a bit bewildered and that.

Amy I suppose. I told them to tell Gabriel too. Now he'll be the one that's bewildered. (*After a pause*) He said I was callous. (*Surprised*) It's true . . . I am. Well, a bit. (*Puzzled*) I never used to be.

Arthur Probably were, mate. Just didn't realize it. Everybody is.

Zoe (*reprovingly*) Buddha wasn't, Arthur.

Arthur Oh come on, Zo. All those Zen stories you're always reading. What about that one with the teacher holding the stick over the bloke's head. "If you say this stick is real, I'll hit you with it; if you say the stick's not real I'll hit you with it; if you don't say anything I'll hit you with it."

Zoe Yeah, but he's not being callous. That's about how he's trying to enlighten his pupil. He's teaching him. He's trying to make him see the alternatives, Arthur. Like how the pupil could grab the stick.

Arthur Okay. Say the pupil doesn't get it. Doesn't grab the stick. So he says the stick's real because he believes that it is. The teacher's going to hit him?

Zoe No! (*After a pause*) Well, yes, I suppose he would.

Arthur (*mildly*) So. You have to be callous to hit somebody over the head with a stick. (*Looking through the papers; absent-mindedly*) Everybody is. One way or another. The way most people are is like they say "turning a blind eye". You have to. You take a real look, just one look at all there is going on in the world and you wouldn't see who you had

Act II

the right to stay alive . . . all that happening to all those people all over the place. So you don't look.

There is a brief silence

Amy *(getting up)* Well . . . I should go, I think. It's after midnight.
Zoe *(going to pick up the tramp costume off the bunk)* You going to take all your gear with you, Amy? I can pack it up in a plastic bag.
Arthur No. Leave it here.
Amy Am I finished with it?
Arthur Dunno yet. We'll see.
Amy I'll miss it.
Zoe You were very good. Smashing. "Think you're so clever! Think you're so clever!" It's a shame you didn't get your picture in the papers that time outside the Houses of Parliament.
Arthur Oh yeah? Supposing somebody recognized her? Lock her up in the bin straightaway. *(He gets up and helps Amy with her coat)* You think the old tramp's worse than that Lena was, Amy? The trick cyclist's wife?
Amy Worse? I don't know what you mean. What do you mean?
Arthur Doesn't matter.
Amy *(thoughtfully)* I think I actually hated Lena, you know. I used to think if you have to be a woman at least do it properly. There wasn't any need for her to look like that. It's easy enough to look female . . . any fool can do it. *(After a pause)* That's callous, too. Speaking ill of the dead.
Arthur If who has to be a woman?
Amy Anyone.
Arthur Any fool do you mean?

Amy looks at him. She goes to speak but stops

Zoe I always get lost you two talking. The Underground'll be finished you know, Amy.
Amy I'll get a taxi.
Zoe Be seeing you then, Amy.
Amy Yes. Goodnight, Zoe. Goodnight, Arthur.
Arthur Night, Amy.
Zoe Tada.

Amy goes out

Arthur stacks up the papers on the table. Zoe takes off her djellabah. She is wearing a pair of boy's pyjamas underneath. She climbs up on to the top bunk and sits cross-legged

You know what I think about sometimes, Art?
Arthur *(abstractedly)* No, what?
Zoe I think—what if I didn't have a brother!
Arthur Well, you do.
Zoe Yeah, but listen! Pretend like . . . like it's my very first time in

London. And what I do is, I ride around and around on the Underground. I'm all alone and I'm always looking. I never stop looking.
Arthur (*grinning*) Here we go.
Zoe No wait . . . wait! I'm as sure as anything that one day I'll see somebody who has my exact same face only he's a man, see. And that would be my long lost brother.
Arthur I haven't got your exact same face. Very first time in London? You were born here.
Zoe I know, I know. I'm just saying how it could've, Art. Or . . . or maybe it would be in some kind of foreign embassy. I'm the ambassador's daughter, see, and there's this big party . . . all music and champagne and everything. And all of a sudden this terrorist comes running in—that's you, Art—with a gun! Somebody screams and then it all goes silent and him and me stare at each other. Fantastic! It's just like we were looking in a mirror! My brother what got stolen by gypsies when he was a baby!

Arthur laughs, puts down the papers and goes over to the bunks

Arthur Shut your face and get under the covers. Story time is over for the night, okay? (*He tucks her in*)
Zoe (*cheerfully*) Okay.
Arthur (*kissing her forehead*) Now, go to sleep.
Zoe (*meekly*) Yes, Arthur.

He sits on the bottom bunk and takes off his trousers and shirt

Zoe (*sitting up*) You never said if I was good at Amy's house tonight.
Arthur Well, you were. I wouldn't have recognized you myself.
Zoe (*delighted*) Honest?
Arthur Straight up. You were supposed to be a tart. Right?
Zoe Well, yes and no, Arthur. It was a little bit complicated. The way I worked it out I was a nice middle class girl ran away from home and got in with a terrible crowd down Piccadilly. That's why I was talking all rough and filthy like that to fit in with them. Pretending to be a tart, more.
Arthur Oh right. You ever think of going on the stage, Zo?
Zoe No. I don't like plays. They're never as good as what you've got in your head.
Arthur (*good-naturedly*) Maybe your head.

He goes and turns out the light. Black-Out

Zoe Art?
Arthur Yeah?
Zoe Is it going on much longer?
Arthur A bit probably, yeah.
Zoe I like Amy.
Arthur (*surprised*) So do I.
Zoe There's nothing bad going to happen is there, Art?
Arthur Go to sleep, Zo.

Act II

In the darkness "Thus Spake Zarathustra" is playing loudly

Zoe and Arthur go out

The Lights come up stage left which is bare with the exception of a small radio which is on the floor upstage

Cissy stands downstage centre with her back to the audience and her arms outstretched from her sides. After a moment she drops her arms, turns stage right and walks a few paces and then stops. She turns to face stage left.

Amy comes on stage right and the two of them drop to their knees and begin crawling towards each other, patting the floor as they go. When they meet at the centre they nod gravely to each other and go on

Gabriel, carrying a suitcase and coat, comes on upstage unseen by them. He stares at them in astonishment and then rushes out

Cissy and Amy go out

Gabriel rushes on again, pulling Lawrence after him. They both stop and stare and then Gabriel strides over and stops the music by turning off the small radio

Gabriel (*tensely*) I don't think I can stay here any longer, Lawrence. I'll have to go home.

Lawrence I don't understand. Where's all the furniture?

Amy comes on carrying a chair

Amy Oh you're back. Hello. How was Brighton?

Lawrence Fine. Well, it rained.

Amy What a shame. (*She puts the chair down*)

Cissy comes in with some newspapers

Cissy (*to Amy*) Yes?

Amy Yes.

Cissy (*seeing Gabriel and Lawrence*) Oh hello. Did you have a nice time? (*She starts tearing the newspapers vigorously into strips*)

Gabriel (*nervously*) Yes thanks.

Lawrence It rained.

Cissy How extraordinary. It was hot here. (*She takes some of the strips to Amy*) Well, what do you think of it?

Gabriel The weather?

Cissy No, the carpet. Don't you think it looks splendid?

Amy goes out

Lawrence (*with relief*) You've been washing the carpet!

Amy comes on with a small table

Amy Yes. It's our last spring-cleaning job. Will you two give a hand with the furniture? It's all in the dining-room.

Amy and Cissy start folding up the newspaper strips and putting them under the legs of the furniture

Lawrence Of course, of course. (*Jovially*) So you've been busy putting the house in order have you?
Cissy Yes, we've done everything. It's the best spring cleaning we've ever done isn't it, Amy?
Amy (*cheerfully*) Yes. It makes you think of the seven devils doesn't it?
Lawrence The what?
Amy You know. In the Bible. That parable. Somebody cleaning up their whole house and making everything neat and tidy and looking absolutely right. And when it's all done, behind them the seven devils come in.
Cissy (*distressed*) Oh Amy . . .
Lawrence (*starting to move; heartily*) Well, you'll need five more. You've only got Gabriel and me so far.

Lawrence goes out

Cissy I always find the parables rather nerve-wracking.
Gabriel (*irritably*) Why is it like the seven devils?
Amy Oh I don't know. (*As if speaking to herself*) I always think that parable's about when you think you're in charge it's just when you aren't. You've got it all under control and everything's in the right place and the whole thing makes sense . . . and that's when they come creeping in the back door.

Arthur comes on quietly and sits in the chair. Lawrence comes back with a chair and he and Gabriel and Cissy are all silent for a moment looking at Amy. Gabriel goes out.

Arthur You've got them all feeling bad again.
Amy I didn't mean to. I was only thinking out loud.
Arthur I expect they'd thank you to keep your thoughts to yourself. They do.
Amy Yes.

Lawrence puts his chair down and goes out. Cissy resumes putting paper under the legs. Gabriel comes in with a chair, stops, and looks at Amy who is folding paper

Gabriel What does she know about devils? Seven? Seventy times seven devils howling at my back on the beach at Brighton last night. Amy. Aimee. Loved. She was the one who saved Lawrence. I tried, God knows, but I couldn't have done it. And last night Lawrence saved me. (*To Cissy*) Where does this go?
Cissy Oh. Over there, thank you. I do wish I could get this song out of my head. It just goes on and on, round and round every time I look at him. (*Sings*) "Blow Gabriel blow, come on and blow, Gabriel, blow." Oh dear. It worries me that I might sing it out loud by mistake.

Lawrence comes on with a desk

Act II

Lawrence Amy is doing voluntary care work with ex-mental patients. (*After a pause*) Amy is doing voluntary care work with ex-mental patients. Why is that any less or more believable than Gabriel last night in Brighton? Running across the beach in the dark toward the sea. Stumbling and sobbing and shouting things I couldn't understand. Gabriel . . . could you give me a hand please?

Lawrence goes out

Gabriel Right. (*He starts to go*) Lawrence isn't likely to speak of it to Amy. We didn't speak of it to each other even while it was happening. Or after. Amy has her secrets and now Lawrence and I have mine.

Gabriel goes out

Cissy and Amy go on putting the newspaper under the legs

Amy This is a rather lonely silence.
Arthur Well, if you'll pardon my saying so, you're all rather lonely people.
Amy If you were really here you could explain things to them.
Arthur No.
Amy (*sadly*) No.

Gabriel and Lawrence come on carrying a sofa

Cissy Two men carrying furniture into a room and two women crawling about on the floor. And somewhere out there the boa constrictor lying on the dry river bank and the donkey whimpering. I don't suppose I'll ever get that out of my head.

Gabriel and Lawrence place the sofa and Lawrence goes out

Gabriel Of course I was extremely drunk. Which means it can be cancelled out. The last time I was really drunk was when I proposed to Lena in the Kardomah Cafe in Tottenham Court Road. And she was eventually cancelled out too.

Lawrence comes on with a small table on which there is a tray of drinks and glasses

Is that the lot, Lawrence?
Lawrence Yes, that's it. What I felt was amazement, primarily. Everything suddenly reversed. I? Holding Gabriel back? Begging *him* not to die? Staring straight into my eyes but I knew he didn't even see me. The rain and the sea and the sound of the band out on the pier playing "Goodnight Ladies".
Amy I can remember walking down Broadway once in New York. It was a surprise to find it such an unhappy, dirty street. There was a young black boy of about fifteen lying unconscious on the pavement . . . a little pool of blood around his head. And a very old black man kneeling beside him. Everyone just walking past. Then a car pulled up and a man leaned out and said "What happened to the kid?" And the old man stood up and said "This boy never did nobody no harm".

Arthur Why remember that now?
Amy Are there rules about when you remember things?
Arthur Certainly. Ask Gabriel.
Amy Not now. He's looking rather sealed off. (*To Gabriel and Lawrence*) Thank you. Thank you both.
Gabriel Not at all. Is there anything else you'd like? Except my life, except my life, except my life. Dear God there is almost nothing now that comes into my head that isn't either sentimental or pretentious.
Amy I don't think so, thanks. Lawrence, why don't you get us all some sherry? We'll be finished in a moment. Surely this is quite an ordinary peaceful scene. Nobody doing anybody any harm.
Arthur Always hard to tell, that kind of thing. The last condition being worse than the first the way it so often is.
Amy The what?
Arthur In the Bible. Your seven devils parable.
Amy Oh. (*After a pause she continues sadly*) Yes.
Lawrence (*taking a glass of sherry to Cissy*) Sherry for you, Cissy?
Cissy Oh yes please, Lawrence.
Lawrence (*getting sherry for Gabriel and then taking it to him*) He's obviously back now to being what he always used to be. He's got that slightly astringent look on his face. Always made me feel I was probably being sentimental or pretentious.
Gabriel I could say to them . . . let's set fire to this house and just go on standing quietly here while it burns down.
Cissy We're very quiet all of us. Although if one could hear thoughts I expect the room would be full of noise.
Amy All done.

They are all standing in a formal pattern and they raise their glasses and sip in unison. Arthur starts to go out

    Arthur.

Gabriel, Cissy and Lawrence stand silent and still

Arthur (*stopping*) Yes?
Amy Are you writing a book about us?
Arthur You never asked me that.
Amy No.
Arthur What . . . "Rocking the Middle-Class Boat"? That the title? Eh?
Amy When I met you that night in the snow you were taking photographs of our house.

Arthur walks between and around in front of them as he talks

Arthur Well . . . (*Sighing*) You know, Amy. You move around. Look at things. Write things down. (*Bleakly*) Gabriel's causes, eh? Which one? Which one? Buddhist monks setting themselves on fire in the market square? Those pictures you see in the Sunday papers? Little babies. Balloon bellies, pipe cleaner arms and legs, big wise heads? The bomb going off in the supermarket . . . some old woman getting her hands

Act II

blown off? Young terrorists hanging themselves in their cells come to that. Yeah? Well . . . I don't know. I don't know. The lace stiff with heavy blood? The flames? The screams? The sudden knife? Loss? Pain? Terror? I don't know. (*After a pause*) The life and death of a butterfly in a day might be enough. If it's a book you want. (*He starts to go out again*)
Amy Wait, Arthur.

Arthur stops

Is that what you would say . . . all that?
Arthur (*laughing*) Oh come on, Amy. I'm not here.

Arthur goes out

There is the sound of "Für Elise" being played badly on a piano

Amy (*after a pause*) The same room. The same people. The sun coming through the window and the little girl next door practising "Für Elise" on the piano. I don't see why anything bad should happen.

The doorbell rings suddenly and insistently and Amy, Cissy, Lawrence and Gabriel start

I'll go.

Amy goes out

Cissy (*nervously*) I expect it's the milkman wanting to be paid.
Lawrence (*smiling and nodding*) Or a parcel.

The music stops

Zoe comes on dressed as a schoolboy. She is wearing a blazer, a rather grubby white shirt and school tie, grey trousers, scuffed black shoes and steel-rimmed spectacles

Zoe Lady said to tell you she was off out for a bit.
Lawrence Oh . . . er . . did she?
Zoe That's right. (*Sitting*) Didn't say where.

Lawrence, Cissy and Gabriel look at her non-plussed

Gabriel What can we do for you?
Zoe You wouldn't have a Pepsi would you?
Cissy I'm afraid not. Er . . . would you like a glass of milk?
Zoe No, ta. I hate milk. I wouldn't say no to a cup of tea, though. My Gran says a hot drink cools you down. Real scorcher today, in't it?
Cissy Yes. Yes, it is . . . I'll . . . er . . . get your tea.

Cissy goes out

Zoe (*calling after her*) Two sugars. (*She looks at Lawrence and Gabriel with surprise*) Aren't you going to sit down?
Lawrence (*sitting*) Oh . . . er . . . yes.

Gabriel remains standing

Gabriel Why are you here?

Zoe (*aggrieved*) The lady told me to come in. What's the matter? You don't want me here eh? Not good enough for you? Not posh enough? Eh?

Lawrence (*rising slightly from his chair*) No. No. Why do you ... (*He sits again and speaks carefully*) We don't know who you are, you see. We ...

Zoe (*angrily*) Who said you did? I never said that. I'm not a liar! (*Sulkily*) Anyway ... who'd want to know you?

Lawrence (*helplessly*) I don't know.

Zoe (*unpleasantly*) Well then. (*Looking round*) She's taking her time with that tea.

Gabriel Wait a minute!

Zoe I am waiting. Aren't I? Eh? I'm sitting here waiting. All I said was she's taking her time. (*After a pause she sighs and becomes depressed*) Probably skipped out the back door. Gone to fetch the coppers.

Lawrence (*surprised*) Why? Why would she do that?

Zoe gets up rather suddenly, goes to the window and looks out

Zoe I don't know. How should I know? (*Speaking to herself*) Everybody always thinking you should know things. (*Turning to them she speaks with passion*) I don't know! I never do know!

Gabriel sits down and puts a hand over his eyes

Lawrence Gabriel?

Gabriel does not reply

Are you all right?

After a moment Gabriel takes his hand down and smiles warmly

Gabriel Quite all right, thank you, Lawrence. (*He crosses his legs, folds his hands in his lap and turns to Zoe, smiling*) Now then, young man ...

Zoe (*laughing*) Now then, old man.

Gabriel (*stiffly*) There's no need for impertinence.

Zoe (*contritely*) Sorry, Cocker. It's just you sounded like my P.S.W.

Lawrence Your P.S.W.?

Zoe Yeah. My psychiatric social worker. (*She sits again*) They call them that ... straight up. Psychiatric social worker. He's a funny old geezer. (*Graciously to Gabriel*) Older than what you are. "Now then young man", he says to me. And then he'll rabbit on for hours. Ramble, ramble. I don't listen. He's all right, really. He's just ... well, he's helpless is what I think.

Cissy comes on with the tray

Cissy Here we are. Tea.

She puts the tray on the table near to Zoe's chair. There is a little silver teapot, a cup and saucer, cream jug, sugar bowl and a little plate with two cakes on it. Zoe looks with suspicion and flinches away from it

Act II

Zoe What's this then? What's all this stuff?
Cissy (*pointing*) Tea, milk, sugar . . . and I brought you some little cakes I cooked yesterday afternoon. They're called Maids of Honour actually. (*Downcast*) They're not awfully nice I'm afraid. I can't help thinking they were meant to come out bigger . . . well, taller. Oh what is it? What's wrong?

Zoe has put both hands over her face and is rocking back and forth in the chair. Lawrence gets halfway out of his chair but sits down again. Cissy puts out a hand as if to touch Zoe's head but withdraws it

Gabriel (*standing up*) Stop crying!

Zoe takes her hands down from her face and folds them in her lap. She looks sad

Zoe I wasn't. I wasn't crying, honest. It's only . . . (*To Cissy*) I'm sorry, Missus. I never meant to upset you or anything. See . . . nobody ever . . . I mean my Gran . . . it's just like in a mug. This is . . . (*She leans over the tray and looks lovingly at it, touching the things lightly*) It's like in the films! It's lovely. I never seen nothing like it before. It's so small!
Cissy (*very pleased*) Shall I pour your tea for you?

She puts out a hand but Zoe pushes it violently away

Zoe No! Get off! It's mine isn't it? I'll bloody pour it!
Gabriel (*with intense anger*) How dare you!
Zoe (*urgently to Gabriel*) Wait, will you? Wait. (*Indicating the tray*) I want this! (*To Cissy anxiously*) No offence, Missus.
Cissy Oh. Er . . . none taken.
Gabriel No! It's not right. I can't allow this. We have been . . . invaded by this . . . this lout of a boy. We've put up with all sorts of . . . (*To Zoe*) We have no idea why you're here! We . . . who do you think you are for God's sake?
Zoe (*pleading with Lawrence*) Can I have this tea first, Guv? I'll tell you. I will. It's just . . . couldn't I just pour it? I'd like to pour it.
Cissy He's so young, Lawrence . . .
Lawrence Yes. (*To Zoe*) Have your tea.

Zoe starts to pour her tea, lovingly and carefully

Gabriel Lawrence!
Lawrence (*troubled*) It's my house, Gabriel.
Gabriel (*after a pause*) Perhaps I should go.
Lawrence Please don't go, Gabriel.
Gabriel (*with intensity*) Lawrence . . . I don't know what to do!
Lawrence Stay.

Gabriel looks at him in silence for a moment. Then he goes and sits down, his face averted from the others. He is obviously near to tears but manages to control himself

Zoe (*with a mouthful of cake*) Smashing cake.

Cissy (*pleased*) Really?
Zoe (*chewing doggedly*) Top notch. I mean it.
Cissy (*getting up*) I'll get you some more, shall I?
Zoe No, ta. Really. My Gran made me eat some cornflakes before I come out.
Cissy You live with your grandmother?
Zoe Well yeah . . . when she's there. She gets about a bit.
Lawrence Your parents?
Zoe (*drawing a finger across her throat*) Dead.
Gabriel (*controlling his voice with difficulty*) Where does your grandmother go?
Zoe (*politely*) Bit hard to say to tell you the truth. I used to know. When I was a kid I used to follow her when she went out nights. She didn't know I did. I was a bit silly about being left on my own. Like the West End . . . she'd go there sometimes. Or up Liverpool Station . . . St Paul's round there. But one night she caught me following her.
Lawrence What happened?
Zoe Well, it was Hampstead Heath way. She was just . . . you know . . . settling down for the night. There was some bushes she was getting under and she'd got all her stuff sorted out. She's got this bag. Newspapers and fag ends, bits of old cups, bananas . . . all sorts. Well, she was just going to lie down when she saw me, see?
Gabriel And when she saw you?
Zoe She hit me. With her stick.
Cissy Oh!
Zoe Right across the head. (*Proudly*) I got concussion.
Gabriel (*angrily*) You're making all this up!
Zoe (*genuinely puzzled*) Eh? What'cha mean?
Cissy (*nervously*) Why shouldn't it be true?
Zoe Course it's true. You ask them at the hospital. I got a card still. (*Taking a grubby card out of her pocket*) I never been back. I could though. I got a number. (*Impressively*) They drove me back to our place in a ambulance!
Gabriel Your place? Your place? Do you mean your home? If you have a home why would your grandmother sleep on Hampstead Heath?
Zoe (*surprised*) She likes it. She doesn't mind being indoors sometimes in the daytime. It's just nights. She can't settle.
Lawrence (*suddenly and with a kind of ferocious anguish*) Where is Amy? Where is she? (*To Zoe*) What do you want? What do you want here? Money? Is that it? Did you come here for money? (*He gets out his wallet*)
Zoe (*confused*) Yeah, I did but . . . hang on . . . hang on a minute. I don't get you. The lady said it'd be okay.
Lawrence (*over-riding Zoe*) Absurd, ludicrous story. Why? Why come in here and tell us all this . . . this . . . (*Fiercely*) It's wrong to lie! It's wrong to deceive people! Didn't anyone ever tell you that? Eh? (*Pushing a bundle of notes at Zoe*) Here. Here, take this. Take it. Take it!
Zoe (*backing off*) I only want a quid. I don't want all that. What's the

Act II

matter with you? (*To Cissy*) What's the matter with him? Is he bonkers or what?
Cissy Lawrence, I don't understand you. Why shouldn't he be telling the truth?
Zoe I'm not a beggar or anything you know, mate. I never would of asked but she said. She did! I said, "Could I wash the car or something?" I told her I needed a quid urgent. She says, "That's all right. Just you go in and ask them. They won't mind."

Lawrence peels off one note and tosses it at Zoe and then goes out

(*Picking the note up*) Thanks, Guv. Ta.
Cissy (*taking a few steps after Lawrence*) Lawrence! (*She turns back to Zoe*) It was true, wasn't it? You weren't lying to us.
Zoe I said! I don't tell lies.

There is a pause and then Gabriel nods and smiles very benignly at Zoe

Gabriel (*strolling round the room*) I only knew one of my grandmothers. Very nice woman . . . a little dull. The other one lived abroad. She and my grandfather came to England once to visit us when I was two but I don't really remember either of them. There is a picture actually . . . me sitting on my grandmother's knee in a sort of smock thing . . . with my eyes crossed. (*He looks over at Zoe and smiles again*) Quite long golden curls I had.
Zoe (*politely*) Yeah?
Gabriel (*strolling round a little faster*) It's my professional opinion that my mother wanted a girl. Although she never mentioned it. However. My grandmother. I gather she was a bit eccentric . . . (*He stops and smiles at Zoe*) Although I think she would have been outclassed by your grandmother. (*He starts strolling again*) But there are resemblances. My grandmother went to live in Corsica after my grandfather died. In a cottage. She kept a donkey.

Cissy makes a small sound and sits down

(*Gaining momentum, he is now unaware of the others*) I believe she had a reputation in the village where she lived for being a witch. My father told me once that the people in the village believed that my grandmother had some kind of control over sharks. I had the impression that this grandmother of mine was some kind of hermit. I imagined her covered in hair. I can't think why.
Zoe (*whispering to Cissy*) All right if I go?
Cissy (*nodding; tiredly*) Yes. You go, dear.

Zoe starts out quietly, stopping momentarily to look back at Gabriel during the following speech before she goes out swiftly

Gabriel (*completely oblivious to everyone*) Herbs and magic potions, that sort of thing. I can remember once telling one of the other boys at my prep school about her. No doubt I exaggerated but it did seem rather posh to have a sort of mad person for a relative. (*Pause*) He was horrified. (*He stands still, downstage, facing the audience*) Oh God, that school. Oh God. Even now I find it difficult to believe that anyone of seven could be that unhappy. (*Lightly*) I used to write the most appallingly piteous letters home. "Mother, Mother, take me home. Put me back inside you." (*Pause*) I used to go up to the dormitory every evening after tea and before prep and sit on my bed. Just sit there. (*Pause*) Feeling unendurably sad. I couldn't cry of course. One didn't. Just sat there every evening for about an hour with this heavy sorrow ... this ... I have never felt such total grief. Well, until ... (*He turns to Cissy and sees that she has fallen asleep*) Oh.

Cissy wakes up with a start

Gone.
Cissy Yes. He's gone.

Black-Out

There is the sound of typing in the darkness. The Lights come up on Arthur's room. He is sitting at the table typing and he wears Zoe's djellabah, which is much too small for him, over his trousers

Zoe comes on. She is barefoot and wearing her underpants and the school shirt and tie and unbuttoning the shirt. She is still wearing the spectacles

Arthur (*looking up briefly*) Go all right? (*He carries on typing*)
Zoe Yeah.

She takes off the shirt and tie and, wearing only the underpants and spectacles, she begins to fold up the clothes and put them in the footlocker

Arthur They all there then?
Zoe Yeah. (*She looks around*) Where's Amy?
Arthur Dunno.

Zoe gets a pretty flowered dress and a bra out of the footlocker. She lays the dress carefully on the bunk and starts putting on the bra. She's about to fasten it at the back when she bends over from the waist

Zoe (*to herself*) "Let the bust drop into the cup, madam."
Arthur (*stops typing; looking up and laughing*) Eh? Let the bust what? What'd you say?
Zoe (*grinning with embarrassment*) I said, "Let the bust drop into the cup, madam". I bought a bra once in this posh place when I was seventeen. I wanted a padded one to make them look bigger only it never did really. Waste of money, that. Anyway, in this shop I'm trying on this bra, just standing up fastening it like I do. And she says in this upset way, she says, "No, no, no, madam, please! Lean forward from the waist and let the bust drop into the cup!" So every time I put my bra on, I say it. Sort of can't help myself.

Arthur, laughing, continues typing. Zoe puts on her dress

Zoe What d'you think?

Act II

Arthur stops typing and looks over at her

Arthur (*smiling affectionately*) You going to take up having those specs on all the time?

Zoe (*taking them off*) No. But I like wearing them.

Arthur Why's that?

Zoe (*finding her shoes and putting them on*) I dunno. It just feels nice in there behind them. I'm a bit upset you know, Art . . .

Arthur (*after a brief pause*) Yeah. I know. (*He starts typing again*)

Lawrence can be heard off stage. He gives the impression of being at the bottom of a flight of stairs, as if some distance away

Lawrence (*off*) Hello? Hello!

Arthur stops typing. Zoe turns towards the door

(*Off; closer*) Is anybody up there?

Arthur starts typing again

Arthur Enter Lawrence.

Lawrence appears in the doorway. Taken aback he looks at them nervously. Arthur nods at Lawrence and smiles whilst he continues typing

Lawrence I'm so sorry . . . I beg you pardon . . . I thought . . . (*Then more resolutely*) Where's the boy?

Arthur stops typing

Arthur (*turning to Zoe*) Boy?

Zoe Yeah. I thought I told you. I decided . . .

Lawrence (*interrupting her*) I followed him here. I saw him go in through a door down there in the alleyway. He can't have . . . (*He stares at Arthur*) You're Arthur!

Arthur (*cheerfully*) That's right.

Arthur gets up and goes to Lawrence with his hand outstretched. Lawrence moves abruptly away so that he comes further into the room

Zoe Hello.

Lawrence I . . . er . . . I didn't think anyone lived here. I . . . when I saw him run into the building I . . . I mean . . . this is a warehouse, isn't it?

Zoe Yeah, it is. We been here over a month. We don't have to pay rent is why. No landlord. It's going to be demolished, see.

Lawrence It looks so . . . er . . . deserted. (*There is a pause while he tries to get a grip on the situation*) If you'll pardon my saying so, it must be rather unhealthy living quite so close to the river. (*Hastily*) Although this is a very nice little place. (*He looks round unhappily*) Very nice.

Arthur (*friendly*) Yeah, we do get a bit of mist coming off the river sometimes but it's not too bad . . . being right up at the top here, you see.

Lawrence (*looking at him, dazedly*) I . . . I . . .

Zoe Would you like some tea?

Lawrence No thanks, really. I just . . . (*Looking hard at Zoe*) You're him. You're the boy.
Zoe (*slightly embarrassed*) Yeah.
Lawrence I don't understand.
Zoe (*kindly*) Sit down, why don't you?
Lawrence (*angrily to Arthur*) What have you done with her?
Arthur Pardon?
Lawrence (*getting frantic*) Amy. What have you done with her? Where is she? Is she here?
Arthur No.
Zoe We don't know where she is just at the moment. Honest. Look, I think you should sit down.
Lawrence What? (*Looking uncertain*) Oh . . . yes. (*He sits*)
Zoe I'll do the tea, shall I?
Arthur (*courteously to Lawrence*) Want some tea?
Lawrence (*looking at him, confused*) What?
Arthur Zo could make some tea.
Lawrence (*standing up and staring at Zoe*) Zo? Zoe?
Zoe Uh . . . yeah.
Lawrence The sister.
Zoe Yeah. (*Very politely*) Listen, I'm sorry being so rude that night at your house. I hope I didn't upset your sister.
Lawrence (*closing his eyes*) I haven't got a sister.
Arthur (*reprovingly*) That's Amy's sister, Zo.
Zoe Oh yeah. Sorry. I forgot. (*Cheerfully to Lawrence*) Always getting stuff wrong. What about that tea?
Lawrence (*with a slight effort*) Would there be . . . er . . . would you have anything to drink at all?
Zoe Oh, I don't know. I don't think we . . .
Arthur Yeah.

He gets up and fetches an unopened half-bottle of Scotch out of a paper bag in the corner

Arthur Get a glass will you, Zo?
Zoe Right. (*To Lawrence*) Water?
Lawrence What? . . . No . . . er no thanks . . . just . . .
Zoe Righto.

She takes the bottle from Arthur and goes out

There is a silence

Lawrence I find myself wanting to say "She is all I have" . . .
Arthur That's okay. I know she is.
Lawrence (*angrily*) Look . . . if you don't mind! (*Both imploring and angry at once*) Don't mock me! I couldn't . . . (*Rapidly. Embarrassed but forcing himself on*) I don't know why I came here. I suppose I thought the boy could lead me to . . . I hid outside the house behind the hydrangeas. When he . . . she . . . So I just followed. Then this place . . . I've never been in this part of London . . . I . . . As a matter of fact I was a bit

nervous about running into the grandmother . . . (*He looks at Arthur quickly and then away again*) Oh God.
Arthur Amy isn't here. She really isn't.
Lawrence (*loudly*) But she is sometimes, isn't she? Often! Often!
Arthur Yeah, she is.
Lawrence What I want to say to you . . . I only want to try to . . .

Zoe comes on with a drink

Zoe (*handing him the glass*) Here we go.
Lawrence Oh thanks . . . thanks very much. (*He drinks it down in one go, chokes, and after a pause*) I shouldn't have come.
Zoe Oh listen. You're very welcome. You are.
Lawrence (*looks at her with some pain*) Please. (*After a pause*) Please . . . (*Carefully to Arthur*) I don't understand it, you see. I don't have to understand it, I realize that. There have always been a . . . (*After a pause*) . . . a great many things I didn't understand. (*He attempts to laugh*) Difficult to put my finger on much of anything I . . . Oh God . . . (*Pause and then he continues matter-of-factly*) For example. When I was thirteen I decided I had a vocation. My parents were overjoyed. So I was taken out of school and sent to a seminary up north. I was amazingly happy there. Everybody seemed entirely pleased with me. Then one of the priests raped me. Foolish silly business . . . (*Pause*) Poor fellow. But I cracked up very badly. Decided I was contaminated. Evil. Outer darkness . . . that sort of thing. Ludicrous attempt to hang myself . . . Home to my parents. More or less put back together again by an awfully nice old German psychiatrist. (*Pause*) They sent me to a farm in Wales to . . . convalesce or recuperate or whatever. I fell in love with a young heifer. Beautiful creature. (*Pause*) So beautiful. I used to make love to her every evening in the barn. From the back the way you do. Against the law of course but I never thought of that. It simply never occurred to me. Afterwards when I walked away from her out of the barn she used to watch me over her shoulder. Her eyes . . . (*Pause*) I think she loved me too.
Zoe (*warmly*) She did. I bet she did.
Lawrence (*to Arthur*) I don't know why I said all that. I've never told anyone before. Never.

Arthur smiles at him and nods

(*eagerly to Arthur*) Listen! The thing about Amy is there's never been any of that . . . that darkness or confusion for her.

Amy comes to the door unseen by the others. She is holding a bunch of wild flowers and grasses and stands listening

Arthur Never?
Lawrence No! No! There's a marvellous kind of serenity about her . . . like the moon. You know all those awful ridiculous doubts that one has? Not Amy. She's clear. She's . . . she's selfless.
Arthur Selfless?

Lawrence Oh yes! She always the other people first. She doesn't make demands, she simply accepts. Everyone. Me. That's *why* . . . that's why she's loved.

Amy comes into the room

Amy How dare you! How dare you come here, Lawrence? How dare you!
Lawrence I was looking for you.
Amy You shouldn't be here! (*To Arthur angrily*) Why did you let him?

Arthur shrugs mildly

Zoe Amy, we . . .
Amy (*furiously to Zoe*) You heard what he said. Loved? (*Throwing the flowers on to the floor*) Loved?

Black-Out

Out of the darkness there is the sound of weeping. The Lights come up on Cissy and Gabriel in the living-room. Gabriel is sitting on a chair weeping uncontrollably. Cissy, wearing her dressing-gown, is standing awkwardly near him

Cissy Oh don't Oh please don't. Please don't cry.
Gabriel Shut up! For Christ's sake just shut up!

Cissy flinches and walks away from him. He gets up

Oh God, I . . .
Cissy (*brightly*) It's quite all right, really. It's . . .
Gabriel I'm sorry I shouted at you, Cissy. It . . . it isn't anything to do with you.
Cissy (*retaining the brightness*) Oh . . . well I think it must be, you know. Something to do with me. People do. Quite often they . . . I think it must be something I do without knowing I do it.
Gabriel Cissy, I hope you'll pardon me. I've . . . been under a good deal of strain recently.
Cissy Oh please. There's nothing to pardon. Truly. Lawrence told us that you were . . .
Gabriel Cracking up?
Cissy (*embarrassed*) Well . . . I'm being very selfish talking about myself when you . . . Forgive me.
Gabriel You are an extraordinarily nice woman, Cissy.
Cissy (*quickly*) Oh no! I mean it's awfully kind of you to say so but I can assure you I . . . (*After a pause she continues sociably*) Do you know, there have been times when I've thought of going to see a psychiatrist myself? Silly, because there's nothing the matter with me . . . I'm just a very untidy disorganized person. But I get these pictures . . .
Gabriel Pictures? What kind of pictures?
Cissy (*embarrassed*) Oh they're just . . . you mustn't trouble yourself about me, Dr Foster . . . Gabriel. I'm perfectly all right really . . . you're the one who . . . (*After a pause*) I wish there was something I could do to help.
Gabriel You could tell me about your pictures. Take my mind off myself.

Act II

Cissy (*backing off*) Oh, I don't think I . . . I've never . . . (*After a pause*) Well . . . (*Taking courage, she looks at him*) They're really quite absurd sometimes. I don't get them all the time of course. Only when I'm very tired and can't get off to sleep. I've no doubt it's all got to do with my metabolism. (*She laughs nervously and then continues rapidly*) Well . . . for example . . . birds. Very big black birds. Like huge ravens. Walking about . . . only they're . . . er . . . covered in something dreadful, I don't know what. Their feathers all matted up and . . . and snarled with something heavy and sticky and . . . and vile . . . (*Quickly*) And then you see, you feel afraid. Well, I do. Or it could be something quite harmless. Even beautiful. Like leaves and flowers and berries all tangled up together. Then you see the face which was there all the time, of course. Hidden behind the flowers and the leaves. Evil, piercing eyes, staring at you . . . (*Quickly again*) If you can keep your eyes open of course . . . but then the moment you close them again the pictures come back . . . only different. (*Pause*) The worst one . . . the worst one of all . . . I can't remember when I had this one. Not long ago. I can't remember. Sand dunes. Pale gold sand and a blue sky. Such a feeling of peace . . . all that space and silence. And on the sand there are lines . . . er . . . drawing themselves. I mean marvellous patterns of lines just appearing . . . hundreds of them. And suddenly realizing (*Becoming agitated and distressed*) . . . suddenly . . . that the lines . . . the lines . . . (*She tries to control her rising emotion*) The lines are being made by babies' fingers, you see. Babies trapped under the sand. Trying to get out.
Amy (*off; calling loudly*) Cissy? Cissy!
Cissy Oh!

Amy appears at the door

Amy (*shouting*) Cissy! Where are you?
Cissy I'm here! I'm here! What is it, Amy? What's wrong?
Amy (*angrily*) I'm leaving Lawrence.
Cissy Amy!
Gabriel What are you talking about?
Amy (*rapidly and unpleasantly*) I should have thought that was fairly clear, Gabriel. Even to a schizophrenic psychiatrist. I—Amy—Leaving—Lawrence. Have you got that now, Gabriel, eh?
Cissy But, Amy, why? Why?
Amy (*sighing*) Oh Cissy, how silly you are.
Cissy (*humbly*) I know.
Gabriel Why silly? What's silly about that? You barge in here bellowing about divorce. What other question is there? Why?

Amy looks at him and laughs

Amy Lawrence told me what happened in Brighton.
Gabriel (*outraged*) He should not have told you!
Amy (*laughing derisively*) Really, Gabriel! Pounding down the beach into the sea! You must have looked ridiculous. Both of you. Absolutely ridiculous.

Cissy (*imploringly*) Amy! Amy!
Amy (*nastily*) Oh come on, Cissy, it's very funny. Gabriel shouting and swearing. Crying too, I'll be bound. Did you cry, Gabriel? And Lawrence pattering along behind him. "Stop, stop, Gabriel! Please don't kill yourself!" (*Fiercely impatient*) And the moon bored to *pieces* by it all!
Gabriel (*starting to move away*) My God!
Amy How stupid you are . . . both of you! The greed! You'd take up the whole sky, you two, with your ludicrous suffering if you could. Out of the way, stars! Shove over moon! Gabriel and Lawrence are in despair. Little boys kneeling at the foot of their coffins! Oh yes! And in the distance . . . on the *edge* of it all . . . the women, the chorus of women, lifting up their voices and weeping for you. Balls, Gabriel! It's all balls!
Gabriel (*shouting*) Shut up! You're talking like a maniac!
Amy (*shouting*) You should know . . . psychiatrist!
Cissy (*loudly*) *I* know!

They look at her surprised

(*quickly*) Tea. A nice cup of tea. I'll make us some tea and then we can all sit down quietly and . . . (*After a pause*) Amy, please, please stop.

Zoe comes running on

Zoe You all right, Amy? I was worried.
Amy (*snapping*) Why?
Zoe I was afraid maybe you'd . . .
Amy Yes?
Zoe Uh . . . do something.
Amy (*exasperated*) What? What would I do?
Zoe (*embarrassed*) Well, you know, Amy . . . something bad maybe . . .
Amy (*turning away*) Oh my God!

Arthur and Lawrence come on. Arthur is dressed in ordinary clothes, as in Act I, and he carries the flowers

Arthur Zo!
Zoe Oh Arthur . . . I shouldn't have run after her.
Arthur No, no. It's all right. It's okay, Zo.
Cissy Lawrence! Who are they? Why are they here?
Lawrence It's all right, Cissy. They're friends of Amy's.
Gabriel Friends!

Arthur goes to Cissy and holds out his hand

Arthur (*in a very friendly manner*) We haven't really met. You're Ann, aren't you?
Cissy (*staring at him, then taking his hand*) Yes. Yes, I am.
Arthur (*smiling*) How do you do.
Cissy How do you do. (*Simply*) I hope you'll excuse me but I think perhaps I'll go to bed. (*She starts to go out*)
Arthur Don't go, Ann.

Act II

Arthur hands her the flowers

Cissy Oh. (*She looks at them and sits down*)
Gabriel Amy! Would you be good enough to tell us what is going on.
Amy (*to Arthur*) I have to be followed? I can't be left alone?
Arthur Dunno, Amy. What do you think?
Amy I'm not going to do anything "bad", you know, Arthur. That's not my number. That's for chaps, didn't you know that? I thought you knew everything. I've *been* alone today. I took a Green Line bus out into the country. I had a marvellous time. I like being alone. (*After a pause she continues quietly*) I don't think I can stay here, Arthur.
Arthur Where do you think you want to go, Amy?
Amy Can I come with you?

Lawrence is becoming increasingly agitated

Lawrence (*to Amy*) But you said . . . (*Turning to Arthur*) Was she lying to me? Were you both lying? You said . . . You said you weren't Amy's lover. (*He starts to go*) I can't bear this.
Arthur (*kindly*) Hang on.

Lawrence stops

Nobody lied to you, mate. Word of honour.
Amy (*to Lawrence*) I'm not anybody's anything! Not anybody's!

There is a silence. Suddenly Cissy begins to laugh

Cissy (*through the laughter*) Oh dear . . . it's just the idea of Amy running away from home with a crazy old woman tramp. (*To Arthur*) I keep seeing you in that awful little woollen hat . . . I'm sorry . . . I'm so sorry . . . I expect I'm a little hysterical.
Zoe (*laughing delightedly*) Yeah, but he really was funny, wasn't he? He didn't half look potty.

Arthur good humouredly mimes waving the stick

Arthur (*assuming an old tramp voice*) Silly sods the lot of you. Think I don't know?

Amy joins Zoe and Cissy in laughing at Arthur

Gabriel How can you!

They stop laughing

(*To Amy*) Heartless! You're completely heartless!
Amy I am not!
Gabriel You are. Cruel and selfish and heartless. Amy, Lawrence is a wounded man!
Lawrence (*with painful exasperation*) Don't, Gabriel.
Amy Oh yes. Help the wounded. (*To Lawrence; passionately*) Well, finally you can't. I know! (*Turning to Gabriel she continues lightly*) Oh

. . . actually there is one thing you can do. You know in Paris on the Metro how they have those signs up? These seats are reserved "pour les mutilés de la Guerre". (*Very unpleasantly*) Well, if you want to feel noble and wonderful, Gabriel, you can give up your place on the train to them. And it doesn't do anybody any good at all. Ever!

Cissy (*shocked*) Oh Amy, that does sound heartless.

Gabriel Yes!

Lawrence (*to Amy*) Is that what you did? Give up your place to me?

Gabriel Rubbish! Pretentious rubbish! Lawrence, don't you see how everything is diminished by that kind of ridiculous fifth-rate symbolism?

Amy Oh Christ . . . your intellect, your awful snobbish public school intellect. Why shouldn't what Lawrence said be true? Why not?

Gabriel Because I say it isn't!

Amy And who are you? The Holy Ghost?

Gabriel (*after a pause*) I'm going. I shan't come back. (*He starts to go*)

Lawrence Why? Why are you going, Gabriel? Don't go.

Gabriel (*stopping*) You told her what happened in Brighton. Amy found that uproariously funny. She laughed and laughed. Didn't you, Amy?

Lawrence (*incredulously to Amy*) No, Amy . . .

Amy I was angry.

Gabriel Oh I see. Of course. That would explain everything. Why you've been in and out of this house whenever you feel like it. Vanishing. Abandoning everyone. Bringing all sorts of . . . (*He looks at Arthur and Zoe and looks away*) Totally irresponsible. A . . . a grotesque transformation from an ordinary, kind, loyal, generous . . . yes, I would say generous woman into a . . . a . . .

Amy Monster?

Gabriel Yes, if you like, yes!

Amy That's not fair.

Gabriel Fair, Amy? Fair? That night in the snow when you talked about something "going on" for you. Since then you've behaved as if nothing was going on for anyone else. You also mentioned suffering. Well that goes on too. Ask your sister!

Cissy (*getting up*) Oh, please. Don't.

Gabriel (*to Cissy*) I'm sorry. I was only trying to . . . (*To Amy*) Amy, do you think you're *alone*? Do you think you are the only one there is?

Amy Yes. (*After a pause*) Yes.

Gabriel No! What about Lawrence? Before he met you he really didn't want to stay alive. He tried to kill himself once. Have you forgotten that?

Lawrence Twice.

Gabriel What?

Lawrence Once was after I met Amy. The day we found out about no children.

Gabriel (*after a pause*) I didn't know.

Amy Gabriel, on the beach at Brighton weren't you the only one there was?

Gabriel stays silent

Act II

Lawrence Weren't you?
Gabriel (*heavily*) Yes. I suppose I was.

They all remain silent

Cissy (*peacefully*) There was a story our Granny used to tell, do you remember, Amy? About going out for a drive with her best friend and two young men. The girls were put in the back seat and as they drove along Granny's best friend said, "Nobody loves me and my hands are cold". And her young man turned around and said, "God loves you and you can sit on your hands".
Amy (*smiling*) Yes.

Arthur touches Zoe's shoulder and they quietly leave the room unnoticed by the others

Lawrence Amy . . .
Amy Yes?
Lawrence What are we going to do now?
Amy I don't know.

They are silent

Cissy I think I'll buy myself a little house in a village by the sea.
Amy Oh Cissy, you'll like that.
Cissy Yes.
Amy Do you think I should come with you?
Cissy I don't know.

Silence

Gabriel Must you leave Lawrence, Amy?
Lawrence (*gently*) Don't, Gabriel. (*To Amy*) I would like you to do whatever you . . . what you want, Amy. Whatever it is. (*To Gabriel*) Fifth-rate sentimentality would you say, Gabriel?
Gabriel I don't know.

The Lights fade slowly to Black-Out during the following

Amy Arthur says everyone is callous. One way or another. He says, "The way most people are, is, like they say, turning a blind eye. You have to", he says. "If you take a real look, just one look at all there is going on in the world you wouldn't see how you had the right to stay alive. All that happening to all those people all over the place. So you don't look."

Black-Out. Lawrence, Cissy, Gabriel and Amy go out

The Lights come up immediately on Arthur's room where Zoe and Arthur are packing. Arthur is putting books into a cardboard box and Zoe is packing the tramp's and boy's clothes into a big plastic bag. The last thing she picks up is the tart's wig she wore in Act I

Zoe Art.
Arthur Yeah?
Zoe Could I keep this, Arthur?
Arthur (*looking up; laughs*) Sure, if you want to, Zo.
Zoe And the specs, could I?
Arthur Course.
Zoe Thanks, Art. (*She puts them into the footlocker*)

Arthur comes over and ties a knot in the plastic bag

Arthur We can drop this off at the Salvation Army on the way. (*He goes to the typewriter*) This going to fit in there? (*He picks up the typewriter and takes it to her*)
Zoe Yeah,

She wraps the typewriter in the djellabah and puts it in the footlocker. Arthur is stacking the yellow paper. He folds it and puts it in the pocket of his coat

Arthur You got your passport by the way?
Zoe (*indignantly*) Course I do.

The Lights begin to fade on them

Zoe Think it went all right then, Art?
Arthur Not too bad.

The Lights fade to Black-Out stage right as a rosy-pink light comes up immediately stage left

The music "Für Elise" is heard

Cissy comes on somewhat anxiously wearing a pink tutu and a red clown's nose. She looks uncertainly round the stage as if searching for something. Then, seeing the audience, she turns to face them. Laces her fingers together at her waist and smiles at them

The Lights fade to Black-Out

CURTAIN

FURNITURE AND PROPERTY LIST

ACT I

Essential pieces of furniture:
On stage: 3 chairs
    Sofa
    Small table. *On it:* telephone
    Desk
    Small table. *On it:* small vase containing a rose

Off stage: 3 take-away boxes containing fried chicken (**Lawrence, Amy** and **Cissy**)
    Sewing basket, containing pins etc. (**Cissy**)
    Coffee table (**Arthur**)
    Tray. *On it:* brandy bottle or decanter, 4 brandy glasses, 4 coffee cups and saucers, coffee pot
    4 garden chairs
    Potted plant (optional)
    Amy's coat (**Arthur**)

ACT II

On stage right: 2 bunk beds set against a wall. *On lower bunk:* the tramp's costume
    Door
    Small table. *On it:* stack of yellow paper, typewriter
    Stool
    Bookshelf. *On it:* books
    Chair
    Footlocker placed against the end of the bottom bunk. *On it:* **Zoe**'s wig and part of the costume she wore as a tart. *In it:* **Zoe**'s flowered dress, bra
    Cardboard box
    Large plastic bag
    Half-bottle of Scotch in a paper bag

Off stage: Tray. *On it:* 3 mugs, a pot of honey, a sugar bowl (**Zoe**)
    Glass (**Zoe**)

On stage left: Small radio on the floor

Off stage: Coat and suitcase (**Gabriel**)
    Chair (**Amy**)
    Chair (**Lawrence**)
    Chair (**Gabriel**)
    Newspapers (**Cissy**)
    Small table (**Amy**)

Desk **(Lawrence)**
Sofa **(Lawrence** and **Gabriel)**
Small table. *On it:* tray of glasses, with sherry bottle etc. **(Lawrence)**
Tray. *On it:* small silver teapot, cup and saucer, cream jug, sugar bowl, small plate with 2 cakes **(Cissy)**
Bunch of wild flowers and grasses **(Amy** and later **Arthur)**

Personal: Grubby piece of card **(Zoe)**
Wallet. *In it:* a wad of bank notes **(Lawrence)**

LIGHTING PLOT

ACT I

To open: Full general lighting

Cue 1	Amy: "He's not coming." *Black-out*	(Page 4)
Cue 2	When ready *Lights up on* Amy, Lawrence *and* Cissy	(Page 4)
Cue 3	Amy: ". . . ask anything at all." *Black-out*	(Page 5)
Cue 4	Arthur: "Nothing at all?" *Lights up*	(Page 5)
Cue 5	Arthur takes the telephone and goes out *Lights change to give the effect of bright sunlight*	(Page 7)
Cue 6	Lawrence goes out as Arthur comes on *Lights change to outdoor evening light*	(Page 12)
Cue 7	Arthur goes out *Lights change to blue-white and give the effect of snow falling*	(Page 19)
Cue 8	Amy: "Knowing." *Snow effect stops*	(Page 21)
Cue 9	Amy walks back to the spot where she was standing before Gabriel came in *Lights change to general centre stage*	(Page 22)
Cue 10	Gabriel: "I don't know!" *Black-out*	(Page 23)

ACT II

To open: Lights up on Arthur's room stage right

Cue 11	Arthur turns out the light *Black-out*	(Page 28)
Cue 12	When ready *Lights up stage left on* Cissy	(Page 29)
Cue 13	Cissy: "Yes. He's gone." *Black-out*	(Page 38)
Cue 14	Sound of typing *Lights up on* Arthur's *room stage right*	(Page 38)
Cue 15	Amy: "Loved?" *Black-out*	(Page 42)
Cue 16	Sound of weeping *Lights up on the living room stage left*	(Page 42)

Cue 17	**Gabriel**: "I don't know." *Lights fade slowly to Black-out*	(Page 47)
Cue 18	**Amy**: "So you don't look." *Lights up on **Arthur**'s room stage right*	(Page 47)
Cue 19	**Zoe**: "Course I do." *Lights begin to fade*	(Page 48)
Cue 20	**Arthur**: "Not too bad." *Lights fade to Black-out stage right as rosy-pink light comes up stage left*	(Page 48)
Cue 21	**Cissy** smiles at the audience *Lights fade to Black-out*	(Page 48)

EFFECTS PLOT

ACT I

Cue 1	**Amy:** "Oh yes." Telephone rings	(Page 1)
Cue 2	Lights up on **Amy**, **Lawrence** and **Cissy** eating in silence Telephone rings	(Page 4)
Cue 3	**Gabriel** sinks down into the chair Door slam	(Page 23)

ACT II

Cue 4	**Arthur:** "Go to sleep, Zoe." "*Thus Spake Zarathustra*" plays loudly and then starts to fade after Amy and Cissy go out	(Page 29)
Cue 5	**Gabriel** switches off the small radio Music stops	(Page 29)
Cue 6	**Arthur** goes out Sound of "*Fur Elise*" being played badly on a piano	(Page 33)
Cue 7	**Amy:** ". . . anything bad should happen." Door bell rings suddenly and insistently	(Page 33)
Cue 8	**Lawrence:** "Or a Parcel." Music stops	(Page 33)
Cue 9	Rosy-pink light comes up stage left Music of "*Fur Elise*"	(Page 48)